No Sign of Ceasefire

No Sign of Ceasefire

An Anthology of Contemporary Israeli Poetry

Edited and translated by

WARREN BARGAD and

STANLEY F. CHYET

SKIRBALL CULTURAL CENTER

Los Angeles

For Charlotte Levine

Contents

Acknowledgments

A number of individuals and institutions have had significant roles in making the present volume possible. We owe special thanks to the Center for Jewish Studies at the University of Florida, to the Hebrew Union College–Jewish Institute of Religion, and to the Skirball Cultural Center.

We proudly and gratefully acknowledge the friendship and support of Dr. Willard Harrison, former Dean of the College of Arts and Sciences of the University of Florida; Dr. Uri D. Herscher, former Executive Vice President of the Hebrew Union College–Jewish Institute of Religion and Founding President of the Skirball Cultural Center; Drs. Shaya Isenberg, Hernan and Maria Vera, and Ralph Lowenstein; Leah Schweitzer; Nomi Teplow; Dr. Yaffa Weisman; and Helene Berinsky. It would be very difficult to exaggerate the importance of their encouragement.

Special and very personal thanks are owed the poets with whom we worked over several years to produce the translations included in this volume: Leah Aini, Zvi Atzmon, Maya Bejerano, Erez Biton, Raquel Chalfi, Mordechai Geldman, Admiel Kosman, Yitzhak Laor, Rivka Miriam, and Avner Treinin. We want to express our thanks also to Tami Mikhaeli of ACUM: The Society of Authors, Composers and Music Publishers in Israel, and to the estate of Ya'ir Hurvitz.

Whatever we have achieved would not have been achieved without the loving support of our families:

Arlene, Adena, and Rob Bargad

Geri, Susan, and Michael Chyet—

Finally, we have been dear friends, colleagues, and collaborators for over thirty years, and each of us says to the other *mi-qerev lev rav todot, y'didi.*

Introduction

"A precarious, daring refuge, full of sweet and awful vision"[1]—that is the American painter R. B. Kitaj's sense of Israel. He has in mind a nation, and perhaps more pointedly a society, whose history is nothing less than amazing. A state that in 1998 observed its first half-century of national independence is heir to a millennia of Jewish tradition—among the oldest spiritual and literary heritages in the annals of humankind. Israel's revival as a major center of Jewish population dates back well under a century, but Israeli society has nonetheless managed to take an ancient language used in the main for devotional purposes over a great many centuries and refashion it as an efficient vernacular vehicle for fully modern expression.

The revival of Hebrew as a vernacular is the achievement not of a long-settled Hebrew-speaking community, but—at least initially—of "returnees" from a thoroughly polyglot diaspora. How many Israelis even a hundred years after the debates between the founders of Political Zionism and the exponents of Cultural Zionism can claim Hebrew-speaking great grandparents? So, in a certain sense, it was, *it is,* memory that must be credited with Israel's emergence—a lengthy, tangled memory, to be sure.

But that memory is not rich, or was not rich, in a secular aesthetic— or, to speak in literary terms, a span of belletristic precedents. Jewish historical circumstance decreed that belles lettres, though not entirely absent, would not occupy much of a place in the Jewish people's classical Hebrew inheritance. Modernity decisively reversed that tradition as it did so many other classical norms. In contemporary Israel, belles lettres, not without their large ration of conflict and struggle, are accorded niches of honor in the pantheon of Hebrew culture. Fiction, poetry, drama, criticism—to say nothing of the other arts—mirror a Hebrew-speaking society in which virtually every tendency of modern civilization is to be encountered. There is of course artifice aplenty—artifice primarily, which is to say, *imagination as an indispensable matrix* of what these artists have created—but artifice does not cancel out reality. It is rather that, as Wallace Stevens once put it, "something of the unreal is necessary to fecundate the real."[2]

All the issues, great and trivial, of modern life permeate the literary art of Israel. Global civilization, it might be said, has a home in that art. This is not to suggest that the insistent sense of isolation, of distance, which underlay so much of Israeli writing a generation ago, has evaporated; it has not, but it seems very much attenuated. The focus is no longer so pointedly on national identity, but far more on what the American novelist William Styron, in another but not unrelated context, has called "the frustrating business of muddling through—of making accommodations, of seeking small pleasures amid the heaviness of the daily grind, of somehow getting a little bit ahead; of suffering humiliations, experiencing minuscule glints of delight; of being terrified (or bemused or enraged) by the enigma of existence; of engaging in that old, old quest for somebody to love."[3]

What are the poets represented in this collection telling us about themselves, their society, their world? Though issues of national identity have receded, the same cannot be said for issues of political, sexual, and spiritual identity. The private and the social realms have not gone their separate ways. If the poets and the poetry reflected in this anthology provide any sort of reliable guide, Styron speaks to their situation. But there is more: biblical images, theological and liturgical echoes, historical and mythical references, all of which remain sure channels of art, though the pietist mindset of earlier generations (by no means vanished from Israeli life today) may very well see heresy in their use and manner of appropriation. There does appear to be a residual ideology implicit in these poems; it might be most aptly characterized as one of broad identification with the liberal, urban values of contemporary Euro-American civilization—that civilization and its discontents! Surely that is what moved the senior Israeli poet Haim Gouri to write: ". . . within me there's no sign of a ceasefire, a brief respite, / a breather for the snipers."[4]

Aesthetically, contemporary Israel has proven a nursery of extraordinary productivity. Poetry is still regarded there at minimum with respect and often enough with a measure of enthusiasm unparalleled in the English-speaking world. A robust multiplicity of expressiveness and variegation in style typify the poetic enterprise, as the selections in this volume testify even in translation. When one bears in mind that the country is smaller and less populous than, say, Southern New England, the Israeli achievement assumes an even more impressive shape.

The present anthology supplies additional evidence that Israel is changing, *mais le plus ça change le plus c'est la même chose.* The human paradox has lost none of its might in this Israel already launched into a second half-century.

September 2000

Leah Aini

LEAH AINI, of Sephardic parentage (her father of Ladino-speaking Salonikan ancestry and her mother from an Aramaic-speaking community in Azerbaijan of Iran), was born in Tel Aviv in 1962 and grew up in the southern, poorer precincts of the Israeli metropolis. Today she lives in Ramat Gan with her husband and daughter.

Her voice is surely among the most distinctive to be heard in the world of contemporary Israeli literature. Though primarily a novelist and short story writer—she has published no collection of poems since the early 1990s—she was awarded prizes for the two poetry collections that had appeared: *Deyoqan* (Portrait, 1988) and *Qesarit Hapiryon Hameduma* (Empress of the Imagined Fertility, 1990). A leading personality among Israel's emergent avant-garde and feminist writers, Aini, both in her poetry and in her prose, has created a striking art illuminating aspects of the human experience in Israel that few other poets and fictionists have engaged.

Aini's own thoughts about her work, as she has expressed them to the translators, are worth pondering:

> It's true that in . . . my first books of poetry and prose, I "spoke" more about myself and my childhood environs [in South Tel Aviv], as, you might say, a presentation of my identity card. It's even true that, in consequence, places, people and worlds hitherto unfamiliar (or at any rate [unexpressed] in an authentic voice!) penetrated Hebrew literature for the first time . . . [But] never have I flaunted the banners of poverty, hardship, and misery . . . nor the banner of mizra<u>h</u>iyut [orientalism]!

... I've written poems. I've written prose. I've created a world, real characters, in purely fictional scenes . . . [yet] never have I sought to reflect a reality, social or otherwise, or to convey any sociological-folkloristic message. . . . The Deyoqan poems are about marginal people alienated from Israeli life, but also expressive of universal human situations: deprivation and isolation wherever they exist and, incidentally, bespeaking art!

It is undeniable, as Aini says, that she is first and foremost an artist, not a sociologist or a folklorist. Yet readers will agree that sociology and folklore are not banished from the literary oeuvre she has created with great power of imagination and distinction of style. She is in that respect the heir of the nineteenth-century *litterateurs* who were great artists—Austen, Dickens, George Eliot, Dostoevsky, Tolstoy, Balzac, Flaubert, Manzoni—and at the same time possessors of powerful sociological imaginations. Aini herself has described *Deyoqan's* "Ahmed" as "the first poem to speak of the coming Intifada [Palestinian uprising in the West Bank and Gaza] some two years before it erupted!"

Another presence deserving of special notice in Aini's work—evident here in *Deyoqan's* "Poems ·of a Southern Place," "Survivor," and "A Shower"—is the Nazi Holocaust. She embraces a memory of the terrible fate visited in particular on her father's family in Salonika. The genocide suffered by the Jews of Greece, she emphasizes to the translators, has not been as well known as the horrors the Jews of Poland confronted.

In 1994, Aini was the recipient of the Prime Minister's Prize for Literature. The Prize constituted a recognition that a young artist from South Tel Aviv, the daughter of "oriental" parents, had created—was creating—art of originality and enduring value. Aini's oeuvre indeed possesses a rare vividness and exhibits the sort of quality that V. S. Naipaul, thinking of his own Indo-Caribbean origins, would call "a moral education."[5] Hers is an extraordinary contribution not only to Israeli literature but to the worldwide Republic of Letters.

Perla's Journey
From *Deyoqan* (Portrait, 1988)

Perla blends bluish eyes
with the horizon
a froth of clouds conceals
God have you seen Leon . . .
a sticky coil, black, a magician
a fire-eater to charm her white palms
melting on his way
the flowers on her dress spread in a dizzying
dance around forward
circles widen in the dust
pupils dilating
heavy wind hoops
Perla's slowly burning up

Hunchbacked children stumble on the road
backpacks of books attempting to be forgotten
an abandoned rag doll
a dangling pigtail
a bloody jackknife strikes
dripping with the rust
they and Perla have a language in common
they wipe the laugh's spittle
from her eyes
they stick filthy fingers in the hollows of her body
there's candy treasure there
sticky with sweat and fright
she bites their fairies' cheeks
she picks their ears
she scares off a bird

A bent tree stopped to root on the road
garbage smeared about
psychedelic smells
bottles of emptiness afloat on dry land

Perla pulls them out one by one
she doesn't know all the drunks personally
but lately in a cold greengrocer's glass
Leon is drowning
his mouth stuffed with shells sand and dirt
vintage nineteen thirty
death nineteen sixty nine

In the evening Perla's hut is high
straw sheaves stretched in the wind
harp and flute
Perla's a dimwit Greek goddess
rising from the horizon
her hair's messy, her face red
she extends a long hand
to grab the testes of the vine
a holy angel circles above her
gets caught in the feast of sweet spirits
he whispers to her when
she suddenly forgets
out of sorrow
to ask, to ask—
God have you seen Leon . . .

"Hamasa shel Perla," *Deyoqan*, pp. 6–7

From "Poems of a Southern Place"

1

In this vicinity the cats are especially fat
a boy's painting the gray of a house and wipes his hand with blood
weeds scratch love
in the hands of mesh-dressed prostitutes
there's a kind of etiquette in the stairwell
no one sees anyone else
the sewers are stopped up
but the desolation here is smart
it gets to your heart

5

There
an old man in a flowerpot
was planting spicy greens
with red pepper eyes
he called to me
sweety
come on in.

6

And at the end of "Duties of the Heart" Street[6]
like a crazy man—my brother
barefoot, in a mesh T shirt
plucking strings that refuse to grow up
the guitar's warm bottom
slow dancing at his thighs
Tova the cripple—an audience
screaming gibberish
sun pleasure takes down her undies
Elvis, the Salonika survivor's son
gets her excited
all along her crutches.

Deyoqan, pp. 8–9

Estahor

Backyard Estahor
would sit on a tattered lounge chair
extracting the first bugs of summer
from her sweaty armpits
her remaining black hairs, pulled
back
in a damp Sephardic *kuku*-bun
the first parched noontime
melted the gold hoops in her ears
and the tin shack
with its curtain of Chinese silk concealing
in its cool folds
an Arab with his fly open
only Arabs have open flies
Estahor would cover the folds of
her warm thighs
but three run-over poodles
were the ghostly
spirits of her nights.

"Estahor," *Deyoqan*, p. 10

Ahmed

Ahmed is my urban rooster.
The raggedy man, his face of
thin bristly stubble
his peeling, festering, yellow smile
devilish wickedness knows everything—
Like the sun, but earlier.

Ahmed wakes me up every morning,
when he rolls the trash cans
with a malicious, metallic noise on the sidewalk,
waking all the Jews out of their sleep.
He joins the dawn's barking of the roaming dogs,
the persistent caterwauling.
But Ahmed is my urban rooster.

Across the way, Muhammad, the young garden boy, gathers
the fallen leaves into a black plastic curtain
along with the blossoming of his youth.
His black listless eyes, a look of decay.
Muhammad is always around at the change of seasons.
Always removing last season's remaining stench
and the rest of the Jewish trash.

Muhammad knows in his village no such
flagrant garbage is thrown out so publicly—
like women's delicate, transparent hosiery
which he once retrieved from a crumpled, Israeli trash pile.
Possessed by the plunder, he stuffed them into his pocket—deep.
And the woman soldier goes out every morning on her way to the
    military base
and passes by him, and her soft fingers pinch her nose.
Muhammad just casts after her—a hungry look,
suddenly kindled with black fire.
He reaches his long, persistent hand into his pocket.
Caressing her warm thighs, filling the hose with
an aromatic, feminine, Jewish fluorescence.

Later, when they'd finished—badly
the two would go together to the cold, stinking
garbage room in back.
They take off their rags—
and come into each other
to the sound of caterwauling, the cats looking on
with hungry, cross eyes, glazed from heat.
They crow like proud roosters—
about their healthy, erect maleness, which rises
with a nasty odor to the upper floors.

Musa, the old porter, once passed by there
to pee.
He saw. Fell dumb. Spit furiously—
and turned away, as if crazed—
muttering prayers of supplication from the Koran
and cursing the Jews—
his Arabic mixed with Hebrew
neither one comprehensible.

To this day Musa still does so—
But none of the residents pay any attention.
They just dismiss him with an apologetic smile,
since everyone knows that the children
who run after him down the street,
throw small pieces of stone at him
and call after him: "Crazy Arab," "Crazy Arab . . ."

1982

"Aḥmed,"*Deyoqan*, pp. 11–13

A Blue Cottage

Behind Grandma's house
a blue cottage
burned down with its residents
a stopped-up sink in the yard
and a scorched ice box
a soiled flowered pillow
set out for an airing
appropriated by a ewe untethered
chewing voraciously
on princely roses
that hadn't yet bloomed
I played there
afraid
to hear the nailed wooden soles of
black orthopedic shoes
returning to the cottage
to boil water again in the tin kettle
for the paralyzed old woman in the bed.

"Tsrif ka<u>h</u>ol," *Deyoqan*, p. 14

Survivor

My father's connected to the crucified number on his arm
and listens, listens, as if in tension
in his left ear he's not listening
a reminder of the S.S.'s slap.
With this ear he hears
hears like a mute
but he uses the healthy ear like a hearing aid
for the nightmares that come to him
from Dora, from Buna, from Auschwitz
in hearses
my father cries out once a week as if to say—
I'm all right
and later turns his head on the wet pillow
and falls asleep on his right side
turning his dead ear to my cries
my tiptoeing cries.

"Nitsol," *Deyoqan*, p. 16

Alibi

Don't remember when this happened
I remember a late hard freeze outside
the streets were folding in on me
like black strips of cardboard
a punitive curfew waited in every alley
I was afraid
night in undercover police garb asked for documents
for a joyful lonely walk
I was young
and my soul—
my soul rose from small
empty vials of perfume
my soul fluttered in butterfly buoyancy
into virgin pages
but no male ever received this I.D. card
to let me intrude into his valuable time
and no policeman ever believed the truth that I was
I was young
No I don't remember when it happened
I remember a late hard freeze outside
the streets were folding in on me
like black strips of cardboard
a physical punishing curfew waited in every alley
I was afraid.

"Alibi," *Deyoqan*, p. 23

A Shower

My grandmother combing my hair . . .
to this day joyous combings
sting me into memory

In the small shower stall in the yard
a mirror like a fallen belly
on a wall bulging from the steam
the color of cracked sky
at the side a boiling pot gasping
frothy clouds on the cement floor
the whole sky bathed there
a male cloud and a female cloud
Childhood and I
two by two Grandma put us into
the shower
the touch in this photo I guard
like a dog guards
a bone

Many years later
a man was combing my hair
the touch was soft, soothing,
his hand was warm
bubbles of lust bubbled on it
but it had nothing to do with
cleanliness.

My other grandma
went into the shower alone
without me
(many years before I was born)
her baldness the gas scraped
her fingernails scraped the cement walls
to find heaven

but the Auschwitz heaven
would not be washed
unless my grandma turned into
soap
here too I think
it had nothing to do with cleanliness
but even this picture I guard
I guard it like a dog
and long ago, long ago I buried
the bone of murder
the bone of cleanliness
in the garden of life.

"Miklahat," *Deyoqan*, pp. 21–22

Portrait

Through a portrait of his Polish great-grandfather
I'm learning to look into
the eyes of my new husband
heavy styled furniture
unfrightening mirrors along the wall
a woman of Sefardi roots, uprooted, extinct
at first her hands are smooth dry
she's reflected there
with unabashed chutzpah
the Mediterranean flowers of her breasts
in a cool porcelain vase—
marvelous.

"Deyoqan," *Deyoqan,* p. 28

When We Grow Up

From *Qesarit hapiryon hameduma*
(Empress of the Imagined Fertility, 1990)

When we grow up
I'll build you a sandcastle
and there I'll bake you
the best sand loaves I can.
That's how our lives will be
like the sand[7]
on the seashore
salty and thirsty
and most of the time it's you at the window
it's me at the door
reduced by the feeble hourglass
to spirit, to a dream
we'll see a convoy of sharp-humped minutes
moving off to the height of a date palm
and the Sabbath, suspended from its fronds
refuses to plunge
into the secular.

"Keshenihyeh gedolim," *Qesarit*, p. 18

Marriage

What frightens me most
is that I won't be allowed anymore
ever again
to play hopscotch
on the mosaic of the kitchen curtain
and how we'd scatter in tag
between the parlor porch and the gas oven
and whether I'll ever again have a chance to say:
"Wicked Wicked Witchaleh underpants and shirtaleh"
how could I after we'd played
"Boy Atop Girl."

"Nisu'in," *Qesarit*, p. 19

A Gray Legend

On the morrow of coming years
how will they speak of her?
About the young girl who talked with the gray
birds upon ascent
who flew with her hair among the rooms
her thoughts constantly gnawing
till her soul spilled out of her
who brought her brassiere to catch
a sparrow in her nests
who cast a spell on the cats
who didn't know whether to pounce or to flee

Bands of young boys in soiled T shirts
hid among the trees
blowing life into a stupid clownish kite
she'd sit on the laundry branches
and look at them like an owl
and they stoned her with sentences like these:
Come down, come down, come play with us
for tomorrow you'll be the woman they'll talk about
the one who talked with the gray birds
and she just chirped in anticipated pain
and plucked her feathers with a sharp pair of tweezers
out of self torture and the approaching mating season.

The years passed, stolen.
Of the boys no remembrance remained
only stony males who cast their seed in the wind
and added theft oppression and deceit
and the woman about whom they spoke of because she talked
with the gray birds
they said she was a witch.

But one evening far away, on the morrow of coming years
a woman, her hair gathered with barbed wire
and pins of cane and she, wearing nailed shoes,
went out to gather the laundry that had dried
suddenly she cut the rope
and ascended
a burst of her hair at first was seen as an unidentifiable object
later, an enemy plane, a firebird
till finally it was known as just a common gray
sparrow.

"Aggada afura," *Qesarit,* pp. 21–22

A Woman Rain Drenched

A woman rain drenched
on the kitchen porch
the wind dishevels her sorrow
her hands stroking
the tedium
broom-dragged all day long
lepers
outcast and wanders through her rooms
stones from her eyes are broken
for heels on the sole of her foot
for signs of a man
lost in them
and in the evening she piles upon his bed
from the toy box
from the fragile hardships of
the day-night
like a lead dog leading him
her perfume
along her strangled neck.

"Isha shtufat geshem," *Qesarit*, p. 23

Liquidation

In a Ramat-Gan housewares store
the bitter old lady was
liquidated
she hovered over the customers' frenzy
knocking down kiddush cups
and making noise in the rusting bedpans
her family pushing to sell
a blue Chinese vase
before it shattered by itself.
From the pile I chose a thin red horse
and a candlestick shaped like a child
and with my own hands paid the old lady
who desperately rattled her silverware fingers
moaning in vaporous tears
from the metal kettle
when I came home I read Psalms
and invited the old lady to come for a ride
on the letter-holder horse,
to touch a child
and to light a memorial candle
when she'd see my spirit swinging
on the hands of the old clock.

"Hisul," *Qesarit,* p. 27

At Their House One of the Doors

At their house one of the doors
is always left open
maybe someone will pop in for a visit
from the land of the dead
will stretch out on the child's short bed
and fall asleep
for half an hour, an hour
not more
and they'll come in quietly
and out of breath
wiping off the gray sweat from his forehead
a mole and a worm
feeling alas
one
more time
with clenched frozen fingers
his temples—pounding fiercely
facing the stone
shrieking.

"Beveitam tamid eiza delet," *Qesarit,* p. 34

Rafi (instead of a newspaper notice)

Rafi
how could you go off like that
God dammit
leaving her womb open
begging for a son
would you have to be dragged
such a bad boy
after your first-born older brother?
and who made you a human being
to punish the one who gave you birth
to put out his eyes all at once
on Yom Kippur?
Rafi, David
stop being foolish both of you
your old father is stubborn
insists on seeing you
he won't die
without a blessing,
without the kaddish
in God's name
get back home!

"Rafi (bimkom moda'a ba'iton)," *Qesarit*, p. 35

Zvi Atzmon

ZVI ATZMON was born at Givat Shmuel in 1948. His education includes a B.A. with honors in biochemistry and physiology and he later took graduate research studies in neurobiology. He was a senior editor of several scientific magazines: *Science for Youth* (1984–86), *General Science Newsletter* (1986–90), and *The College* (1986), as well as editor of *Moznayim* (Scales or Balance), a leading literary journal (1989–91). He holds a faculty position for life sciences at the David Yellin College in Jerusalem and is editor of *Galileo—Journal of Science and Thought*. He has served on the editorial boards of the literary journals *Iton 77* (Newspaper 77) and *Gag* (Roof).

Atzmon's first published poems were featured in the literary pages of the weekend newspapers, and his first collection was published in 1981. He has had a large number of prizes and grants for his poetry and has published six books of poetry to date.

His early efforts as a poet reflected a bent toward romantic impressionism. Emotions were projected onto landscapes: the evening sunset, a bit of Ḥayim Naḥman Bialik, and much more of Dahlia Ravikovitch. In many poems a variety of women are available, but the protagonist is timid and self-conscious. He is obsessed by many women, yet his lust is like a terrible heartburn. Love and intimacy elude him. A rare momentary tremble comes alive, but not enough for the harp of Eros.

In the later 1980s and the 1990s, Atzmon turned to other concerns, mostly the politics of conflict and social survival. He explores the taboo of Israel-Arab friendship. His resolve is to spurn the threat of disgrace and use the power of the poetic pen. Many of his works are anti-government broadsides, decrying activities such as the Israeli landgrabs, long-term curfews, racial slurs (Arab hygiene), and the harsh security guidelines. Essentially, he seems to feel that the Palestinian-Israeli situation is hopeless. The Arab communities can look forward only to fear, discord, second-class citizenship and a future of oppression.

Atzmon compares the Palestinians to the Jewish victims of the Holocaust: the ghettoes, the concentration camps, the annihilation of Jews in World War II. These are fearsome experiences which might perpetrate a long-term futile feud between the Palestinians and the Israelis. This horror should never be allowed to happen again, but the threat of endless hostility remains strong. The poet laments that once there was a prideful Israel, but now the State's reputation is sullied by the military occupation that humiliates the Palestinian populace.

In many of his poems Atzmon dwells on the fate of his parents, who left Poland as young _halutsim_—Zionist pioneers, for the harsh conditions of life in Britain's Palestine Mandate and who learned some years later that their families in Europe had been murdered by the Nazis.

Atzmon, like most Israelis of his generation, has seen years of military service. The military experience is alive in many of his poems.

Much of Atzmon's work could be called the "Politics of Aesthetics," a style composed of an abiding sarcasm, a bent toward allusion, and a continual offering of banal but purposeful metaphorical images.

Strong Coffee, the Account
From *Oref* (Neck, 1986)

I want to tell you, my good friend
(I won't mention any name
to avoid stereotyping,
but I will say it's an Arab name)
I'm ashamed, up to my neck in disgrace,
you've got to believe me. You've got to believe
I'm jealous, too, I swear to you, despite
the week's curfew, the landgrabs, the remarks about hygiene,
the search and the language and the orders, the security arm—
you can be hopeful, my good friend,
like a flag on a famous pirate ship,
outfitted with cannon and laden with sweet revenge[8]—
hope doesn't exist for me,
for me there's the knowledge
that only one misstep of the government,
of the chief of staff, or the head of military intelligence, even a
                                    maintenance officer,
a slight error on the map, a total technical blunder,
a misunderstood briefing, a foolish delay in a draft notice,
they'll bequeath me—am I wrong to mention it? am I ill? when I'm
    reminded—
to speak optimistically, only retribution and ghettos and concentration
    camps,
not total annihilation,
not for less than another two millennia.

Now, my good friend, make an account of what you have—
as for me the sum I get is frighteningly simple:
disgrace up to my neck plus bottom-line fear.

"Kafe hazaq, heshbon," *Oref,* p. 32

Black is Solemn and also Signifies Mourning
(Pavanne For an Actress With a Single Syncope)

She's believable, almost good, apparently a prize was rumored,
and once, from up close, real tears could be seen, I swear,
but the masks available are so few, the theatrical accoutrements
at her command, the repertoire she's mastered:
In an agreeable mood she coos "Daddy-leh" to the baby dressed in soft
                domestic lace
her nipples stiffen even when she's not at all nursing,
she digs her fingernails in and bites most amazingly
she moans as if in great agony while her body is lustful and precise,
she laughs, fearfully sometimes, hysterically,
and when expansive, completely free, her face actually turns pitiful,
as if she's weeping, until at last she sprawls, tucks in her legs, holds her
      breath for a time, alarming to one unaccustomed to such feats,
and with her wrist and temples she stills her pulse beats
as the lights
Curtain. *Finis.*

                    "Shaḥor ze ḥagigi vegam shel eivel," *Oref,* p. 35

The Refusal

For Etan

Afterwards we stood in line to shake hands
they said write something, you were a good
friend, what should I have said
he ran to catch snakes, I'd already get them
in jars, a cooler, to use the lab's Latin term,
and it's more like workplace relations,
and in general, I don't like the whole business
with memorial booklets really if you think about it he brought it
                                                    upon himself,
statistically speaking, of course,
and already before the army, with the snakes,
he took too many risks
to suit me and the fact is he had so many
friends but I have none

What am I to write?

"Haseruv," *Oref,* p. 38

Fracture, Half-Brothers, Almost All of Her Died
From Taḥalif (Substitute, 1989)

To her whom we came to know in *The Dead Bride**

Beyond the half-point of my life** I look at
half your body, the suture between you and
yourself, your side that feels and sees.
How is this so: a Siamese twin
whose half-double is already dead.
You know, human deeds are merely an imitation
of something that, on occasion, time or chance maligns.
It may be I was once a bit more,
but the weaker twin is already dead.
When you told me I saw the umbilical cord
and half-brothers, and fragments of a family (the father "stayed with them,"
                              that's how you put it) wounding
with every touch and shred of memory.
I want to tell you, whom else
can I tell: I swear I don't mean it as a metaphor or a quip
just the truth.
A person is born (that's you)
where they were meant to die, all of them.
Now the twin half of my life would have cried.
And what's left to whisper in the ear of your dead half:

Jerusalem, January '86

ATZMON'S NOTES

 * *The Dead Bride* is a play at the Jerusalem Khan on the theme of Anne Frank.
** An allusion to the opening of Dante's "Divine Comedy."

"Shever, ḥatsa'ai aḥim, kim'at kulah meta," *Taḥalif,* p. 17

A Person Against the Pangs of Conscience—
A Case File

Merry with beer[9] and the Greek salad
he went a bit overboard with the tip for the waitress
on whose right leg, ankle high,
around dark skin, limber, like the movements,
hung a chain. Later, when he walked by a
beggar woman, her hand outstretched, filthy, her upper lip
slightly covered the other, mumbling, just a few teeth,
a slight issue of conscience,
let's call it—a dispute between neighbors,
an account settled of the order-size of a municipal law,
                                    or something of that sort.
Come on! let the poor guy live
a little, the same for the old woman struck blind (forgot to mention
      it before),
and for the young high-school girl disco girl from up north[10]
let the world make its way, don't make a fuss,
don't stir up Sturm und Drang
a tempest in a mug of beer or a cup of coins
don't be a nerd, a poet
who stole coffeehouse time from his daughter's mouth
and attention due his family
he squandered on an almost-child-waitress
and the other woman, toothless and timeless, in sturdy workshoes
(this isn't about a blind beggar woman, of course—
another little exaggeration of conscience, maybe a bit overdone).

"Haben-adam neged yisurei hamatspun—tiq diyun," *Tahalif*, p. 19

An Itinerary—Report In a Crowded Meeting

In memory of Dan Pagis

Mr. Chairman, first of all it's essential to weep
and also, demonstrably, to hunger a little, to feel pain, to shake with
    cold

                                when the blanket, thirsty,

wet, the skin tender and sore, to be afraid of the dark, of a dream, of
    your big sister's
stories, of an imaginary snake, of nothing,
to be weak, second-rate,
needy, jabbed with a syringe, tearful,
to be jealous, to move about, needlessly excited, confused, feeling
    clumsy,
abandoned, ostracized, punished without cause, given to tantrums, full
    of rage,
uselessly swearing, to concede, to give up, to be humble, to yield
and lie, to quarrel about trifles, to be stubborn, to be sorry, to be
ashamed to speak the truth, to shriek
(and for reasons not at all justifiable, *slash* really contemptible
slash really despicable *slash* extortion
slash and / or pretense
not to note the dew drops on honeysuckle on an early morning hike,
the shadow climbing up the mountain, the vista, the trail completely
    bathed

                            in a caressing perfume,

a thicket lapping at the shore, hours of ease in the sand, endless
    intimacy)
to find a victim, relief, feeling despicable, driven
from love, humiliated, rejected, lonely
without recourse, mindlessly to yearn, and humiliated
to conjure up a substitute, to seek restitution, to wish, to castigate,
                          and to delude,
to be contrite, to grasp nothing, to pretend, to be reminded, to be
    fear-struck,
to rave like an idiot, to trust
in vagaries to make an effort

without purpose to dread
the edge of the page,
the end. Thanks! I'll
say no more, I'm stepping down, I've run out of time.

What luck. Everything turned
out so well, it's encouraging.

"Maslul—divu'a<u>h</u> bekenes pe-lepe," *Ta<u>h</u>alif,* pp. 34–35

Forty-Two

Forty-two, an ordinary winter morning, then we still said "housekeeping,"
                    today only
a housecleaner, maybe an Arab woman. An ordinary day, humiliation,
                    the fingers yellowed from dishwashing,
from laundry, the harsh soap spells war, I still remember gray tin washtubs,
                    the heart already
soured, shrunken, cold sores even in the land of sunshine!? The key word:
                    humiliation,
humiliation, to put it a bit more professionally—nonfulfillment. A day
                    lost in numbers, ordinary,
unaware, in a land at work, optimistic, proud of attendance, righteousness,
                    carrying on
in a grand history role, the key word: fair, just, only the people are a bit
                    burnt,
a bit extinguished, only the town is ablaze.* An ordinary day, the day when
    her parents
                    died, so many
cousins, infants hung on the wall, to this day, to the end of the whole
    generation,
a few thousand kilometers, one continent, another planet,** the heart
    functions as
                    usual, without
feeling, without murmur or outcry. The key word is not pain but the shame.

Now I want to roll this number around in my mouth, to inspect it from every
                    side,
with my eyes, my brain, in all its aspects, all its parts, even if today
                    is a birthday. Mine. Forty-
two. Before me times two: before I was, always before what I am.

ATZMON'S NOTES

 * Cf. Mordechai Gebirtig, *Unzer Shtetele Brennt!* (Moreshet, 1967, pp. 8–10)
 ** Referring to *Star Eternal*, a book by "K. Tzetnik" (Yehiel Dinur), who describes the most
horrible atrocities in the Nazi concentration camps during the Holocaust.

                    "Arba'im ushtayim," *Tahalif,* p. 39

A Blue Shadow, Two Illusion-Visions
(A non-event in an Army tent encampment)
From *Me'orav yerushalmi* (Jerusalem Mix, 1990)

Nothing to write
in an army tent, awful heat, filthy, swarms of flies,
even worse the endless palaver, ammo in the john,
candy wrappers, jokes for fun, soccer songs,
functioning, the ammo belt, the guns,
a small rip in the tarpaulin
greasy for years, dusty,
torn fibers like a frame
a blue stain, something wholly pure,
an illusion of no-distance, an endless mistake: one or two meters,
that's what you get as you climb onto a field cot, maybe a kitbag, too,
don't close it up, what's wrong with you, where's the rain?
Only an outstretched hand
the touch of a fingertip
holding on for endless hours
stroking the earlobes, the cheek, not saying
a thing, a face you have to peer into, to make out
an invisible angle of your nose
like a slight brown stain on a houseplant
imperfect, but alive, real, breathing.

But the faint shadow of a passing terror
a raven's hop or a late-September cloud:
Why, really, did you ask when we spoke—
diffidence, an utterly academic debate
(the soft blush that caught my eye, was,
it seems, no reason for it),
on the stiffness of the dead man's flesh.

"Tsel tekhelet, shtei mar'ot-ashlaya," *Me'orav*, p. 13

The Psychologist:
A Simulation-Stimulation Game

1—SURVIVAL

You suggest a course on fine cooking:
A gourmet dish—melts in your mouth—panda bear liver,
condor eggs, shall we say, in an exotic sauce, a lingering taste.
You've certainly caught on—it's not simply me,
but a way, a path of tracing, not pursuit,
a rare endangered species.

The argumentation, I admit, is complicated, if you die
of hunger, not merely culinary boredom.

2—OVEREXPOSURE

Can a surgeon love, or have sex
with a woman he's operated on,
who exposed her innards, the inside of her womb.
Can a psychologist, with a woman who's been
his analysand?

3—ALTERNATIVE ENERGY

The gap between things, a geological fault, a crack
you'd say, could be mended
as a waterfall in a potential output of megawatt
literature.

"Ha-psycholog:mishaq simulatzia-stimulatzia," *Me'orav*, p. 11

Forty Days in the Dune. Restricted*

1. PROLOGUE: THE STRIP

> Forty days in the dune, it's like a package deal
> a wasteland, apparently,
> I didn't take a billy club in Khan-Yunis or fire tear gas in Gaza.[a]

2. ARIA: BLESSED IS THE "MATCH"**[b]

> Delicate persuasion, not a law court.

3. MAY IT NEVER END

Smooth and trembling, a woman's back—
the dune breathes, sodden at the soles of your feet.
The line that divides the body's shine from the blue
scatters like hair in windy hours, dizzying, stroking silk.

May it never end
the pure, crystalline sand, the sky,
the silence.

4. MEN IN THE SUN***

But flies about the hut, newspaper corpses,
K-ration trash, a rock station non-stop.
Like a sting the banality swells under
the skin, spreads. From the backgammon board,
rises the burnt odor of killed time,
and the walkie-talkie stubbornly buzzes, like flies:
"Head to pin, Do you read me?"[c]
No comprendo, lamebrain
(the code speaks poetic).

Hot.

5. HAIKU: THE HEAT

Already at ten-thirty
the weapons are red hot, the brain
drips syllables

High Cuckoo

Or a fata morgana:

More Guns

6. FATA MORGANA: ARABESQUES

In the heavy khamsin soldiers of the other platoon
are intent on expelling a second niece of Siham Daud,
pursuing a friend of Michel Haddad's grandson,
beating up the neighbor of an acquaintance of Samih El-Kassem,
handcuffing a distant cousin of Anton Shammas
and looking after their eyes and flooding their ears with "Screwy Arab."
"*Shu ismo* (what's his name), you said?—He knows Hebrew?—Even
    more dangerous."[d]

7. LEGAL COMPOSITION, DARK RED FRUIT[e]
(A sort of children's riddle)

For Sigal

A loaded truck from Gaza.
Fifteen pounds, my God, almost the weight of a child
in a green kaffiyeh, and a ripe, red heart—
a worn simile, if you please, totally lifeless—like blood.
No need for a wild imagination to dry up like the guard unit,
to suffer from hallucinations or whatever,
so as to hear, really hear, from inside the quiet
covering like sand the rush of tires and the echo of dunes,
calls of "Guaranteed!," the swish of a knife slicing
a deep triangle with an expert hand, juice pouring from the corners of
    the mouth,
and a sound of sucking, slurping, white softness like a flag—
innards of large seeds, countless, dark-eyed:
watermelons.

8. INTERMEZZO: CLOUDS ON GUARD

Two ladies in white, arm-in-arm in the blue
quickly converge into a kind of breast that turns,
so easily, into a mustached face
(I swear, it resembles the commander).
A natural Rorschach test for a private.

9. AVE MARIA

And the Madonna's walking around Judea****f
and Samaria,
in the Gaza Strip,
carrying a large basket on her head.

Nostalgia time on Army radio,
Oh, sweet Underground, Russian shirt,
blue shirt.

A really old recording
stuck in the Camps of Sorrow. Apologies to our audience.

10. EPILOGUE: COMING HOMEg

The best songs about the desert,
about the heat, the khamsin that dries up the brain,
will be written in a cool, nicely air-conditioned room

A slight shiver along the spine.

ATZMON'S NOTES

* It is prohibited to pass on the contents of this document to anyone who has no
experience in reading poetry. That's an order!

** Military code.

*** *Men in the Sun* is the name of a novel by the Arab author, Ah'san Khanefani.
Translated by Daniella Brafman and Yaani Demianos. (Mifras [Sail] Press)

**** Composer: Anonymous; Lyrics: Prohibited to publish; Hebrew production:
Lior Yeini (from the record jacket).

a. Khan-Yunis is a Palestinian refugee camp; the violence refers to the Arab *intifada* (rebellion) in the mid- or late '80s and early '90s.

b. The "match" (military code for "soldier") alludes also to Hannah Senesh's poem "Blessed is the Match." Part 3 alludes to Senesh's poem "Eli, Eli" (My God, My God).

c. The italicized words toward the end of the stanza are military code words.

d. Part 6 mentions a number of well known Israeli Arab poets.

e. Part 7 presents a symbolic picture of the *intifada* conflict. The watermelon is green on the outside, white in the rind, and the black seeds also inside. These colors are the colors of the Palestinian flag, its display forbidden in those years. The red pulp of the watermelon is also symbolic of the bloody confrontations.

f. The "Madonna's walking around Judea" was a popular song, among others, translated from the Russian expressing empathy toward the suppressed Soviet population, Jews among them, in the 1970s.

g. *Coming Home* refers to the American film about the Vietnam War experience.

"Arba'im yom bedyuna. Mugbal," *Me'orav,* pp. 20–23

Letters, The Words' Rebellion

Fishing boats—
dark spots bobbing up and down,
held back from the coast until dawn.
The full moon's a white eye patch
on the heart of the sea, an EKG.
The padded steel helmet leaves little to the
imagination.
From the guava orchards a faint smell
of surrender.
Wind-tears in the open, camouflaged patrol car.
Smoke from the huts.
Two camels.
A barefoot old man pulls up a net.
W.T. means Walkie-Talkie, and there's an order,
curfew is curfew.
R.C. means Refugee Camp, you should already know that.
Sign here at the bottom, *dahilakh*, come on!
N.S.C. means Non-standard Billy Club—
just a hoe handle—it's efficient, don't worry—
whack 'em your private number, *ya habibi*, and your signature, too.
Rubber is rubber.
Plastic is plastic.
A tire's burning.
Gas makes your eyes tear.
R.S. means Reserve Service.
And a storm trooper is a storm trooper.

M-o-o-n is moon.
W-h-i-t-e is white.
And t-h-a-t's that. Horrible.

"Otiyot, hitkomemi'ut hamilim," *Me'orav*, p. 25

The Poor of Your City

The poor of your city come first.* Always. A firm principle.
Only the words are pliant. Like jelly.

Of course, your city isn't quite Netanya,
Ashdod, or the border of Holon's mid-street town line: Bat Yam.
Clearly it's a city that's quietly expanding
Metula to Eilat, and in certain circumstances, Brooklyn, too,
Buenos Aires and Odessa.
Not just Jerusalem (the narrow formality of a document)
Beyond the middle of Abu Tor, the slope of Valley Street

And poverty.
There's also the issue of the poor of the land,**, ***
and statistics, a median, and ten percent,
and also—very important—the level of expectations: the past,
     neighbors, a gap.
In any case, the soul—which has much standing among us,
we who know our sacred texts, the Kabbalah and lovingkindness—
always immersed in a kind of famine, a lack.
And who is expert enough to determine
subjective poverty. It's no simple matter.

That is to say: the sector of the city and the poverty line are
elusive, reaching from the heart, my own heart,
my concern, to the race between a glass of milk and a notebook
for a child down the street (mine, only technically),
to the computer club and a comfortable middle-class home
and a once-a-year vacation, not grand,
over which the pondering heart will prevail,
calculating, envious, whose mouth is
the sacred tongue and our sages.

    * Baba Metzia 41a.

  ** Isaiah: 11,4: "And judge the poor fairly and rebuke the meek of the earth"—meaning: the poor of the land.

*** Matthew: 4,5 (The Sermon on the Mount): "Happy are the meek for they shall inherit the earth."

"Aniyei irkha," Me'orav, p. 28

Fingerprinting, A Moment of Grace
From *CortexT* (1993)

A slight hint of wind makes the part
between sleeve and elbow shiver,
the sea's transparent tongue licks, chill air, eyelids and forehead, brings
    back a thought: your toes
wild, far from the perfection of form,
far from the taste of the precision of order.
It's doubtful if they draw much attention from your hands
but nailcutting as a routine
or moments of grace
in my mouth, expectant nipples of
love, the hard skin bitten by my lips,
the heel, gently with my teeth.
Now my palm smooths the sand, steps
that are almost
yours.

"Tevi'at etsba'ot, rega ḥesed,"*CortexT*, p. 5

Prefaces
(A Shroud of Poems)

COVERING THE BLOOD

The dead skeleton[11]
puts on flesh
soft, debased,
growing old.

MY CROWNING GLORY[12]

has fallen
closing her
   bulging
eyes

PARTIAL COMFORT

I, of blessed memory,
am no longer.
Please refrain from condolence calls

WASHING THE BODY

Kaddish [Sanctification]
u-rehatz [washing the hands]
almost like a *seder.*

CEMETERY

— *Shalom,* peace to my dust.
— *Shalom, shalom!* Everything's done. Don't linger.

NAMELY DEATH

But to experience life fully, its essence,
you're obliged to free yourself
of debt, to be free
of constraint, fear, the nightmares that cause you
                              to stray from the main point,

rid yourself of anything fruitless, worth, a bit of dependence,
a fragment of lust, an adulterous erection, bodily pain
or your teeth, peanuts in your mouth, completely free
of the slightest illusion, of the fear of death
that is to say—
to die.

"Akdamot (Takhrikh shirim)," *CortexT,* pp. 18–19

Eighteen Lines of Latter Prophets[13]

Dedicated to the memory of Mordechai Gebirtig
(Born in 1877—Shot in the Cracow Ghetto, 1942)

It won't end well it will end
Remember what I'm saying
Look the smoke is already rising it won't
End well, only this line will be preserved
When all is done, in a trembling hand, the horror will stare right at
Your eyes bulging, our breasts beating in atonement, with a whip, by
    the sword
You'll draw lots, to pull out your hair, and with hair bristling like rats to
    jump and bet on
the waves. But a full wagon wheel no one will save, like straw it will
    creak, eradicate,
shatter, trample, shower, let blood, phylacteries
Prayer will not help nothing will stop the horseman
Won't escape nor will the donkey driver at his back from the snake,
From the lion, from a bereaved bear, it won't
End well. The poem
Now crouches in the shade of a one-day-old tree,
Waiting, sharing with it an open secret, lying in wait in the thicket of
The tiger's heart is planning nothing good
I say this good (Jonah, Nineveh, mountain wine)

It won't end.

"Ḥai shurot nevi'im aḥaronim," *CortexT,* p. 55

Almost Like Me
(A prayerbook forgotten at home,
instead of the Orphan's Kaddish)

So many things I have no chance at all
to grasp, if only at the edge of thought, to approach even to understand
stocks and bonds, economics, or what is the meaning of charisma
—the secret of extended strength like pipes in the ground, under
    concrete roads, stone
fences, and how to manage
these matters, shall we say—at council meetings, how suddenly an item
    of fashion, a
simile created, a metaphor
or a myth, and higher mathematics—a dimension that doesn't even
    really exist,
that's impossible to touch, and knitting, too—threads become a scarf,
not to mention a model or a sweater.
But one thing for certain: My father
horribly thin—veins protruding, a porter
between two businessmen, a senior clerk (the pride of the training
    camp,
Kobrin '37, a frozen photo, a bit artificial, in gray-brown),
a contractor who did very well for himself, and a director of a public
    health clinic
(they all dropped down to the
Land
together, like flies,
without parents, framed sketch, family)
a long surgical scar, a past sealed for the children,
everyday speech an adopted language, endeavor,
a constant toothache, surrounded by bitterness,
a contemptuous critique, demands, sense of nothingness, only the
    slightest of granules

of cigarette ashes—
how did he manage to live
so many years:

49 is inscribed on the tombstone

almost like me.

"Kim'at kamoni," *CortexT*, p. 62

Maya Bejerano

MAYA BEJERANO's parents, avid members of the Shomer Hatza'ir left-wing Zionist movement, emigrated to Israel from Bulgaria. Her father had studied law and been a violinist in the symphony in his home town of Kazhinlak. Her mother, born in Sofia, had sung in a choir and studied to be a nurse.

When they made aliya, everything changed. Her father first worked as an editor at the *Al Hamishmar* newspaper and later became a tractor driver and her mother worked there as a licensed nurse at Kibbutz Ailon, where Maya was born. Maya left the kibbutz in infancy when the family moved through a series of rural locations until they settled at Jaffa in 1954. Later they moved to a more permanent home in 1961 at Bat Yam, a south Tel Aviv suburb on the coast.

After four years at Bar Ilan University, Bejerano moved to Jerusalem to study at the Hebrew University. She served as a teacher of language and literature in a Jerusalem high school, then moved back to Tel Aviv to work as a librarian in Beit Ariela, the central branch of the Tel Aviv public library system. She has worked in this role since 1978.

Bejerano began writing poems at the age of sixteen. Her first published poems appeared in *Akhshav* (Now) in 1972, and her first collection, *Bat Ya'ana* (Ostrich) was published in 1978. A prolific poet, to date she has published eight books of poetry. Her work has been awarded several prizes, including the Prime Minister's Prize twice and the prestigious Israel Prize for the collection *The Hymns of Job* (1993).

In some ways, Bejerano is a follower of the late Yona Wollach (1946–85), a poet whose works are complex, dreamlike, surrealistic, visionary, projecting various types of stream of consciousness and an abiding sense of inwardness. Bejerano has employed these conventions, but her forte is a palpable outwardness. Totally open-minded, she embraces a multiplicity of topics, ranging from the Odyssey, nature, songbirds, landscapes, light, language, Orpheus, street scenes, Geishas, domestic backdrops, art, to ATMs and Stephen Hawking. She has written many erotic and love poems.

Many poems by Bejerano are picturesque, even imagistic, in the sense of highlighting an unconventional structure and syntax. Her poetry calls to mind the idea of naturalism—freedom from preconceived ideas and an impressionistic bent. She is famous for her "Data Processing" poems. To date, they number more than seventy, most of them written in a radical vers libre style.

In September 1993, Bejerano wrote a long essay entitled "In the Poetic Language of the 20th Century," which argued that the time had come for change and discontinuity in Hebrew poetry. She mentioned several mentors: T. S. Eliot, Philip Glass, Jacques Maritain, Marcel Cane—all creative forerunners in their individual realms: poetry, music, film, philosophy, and culture. The plaint, essentially, is that poetry needs to have a new poetic "language," a new way of writing, not the language of academe, but a spontaneous language which would be realistic, unconstrained, guileless, a language offering a simple combination of the poet's "senses and feelings, thoughts and drives."

Recently, Bejerano issued a C.D. ROM featuring poems of hers along with visualizations by Camera Oscura seniors. She has also been translating T. S. Eliot's "Four Quartets" and other poems of his.

Penelope and Odysseus
From *Bat Ya'ana* (Ostrich, 1978)

One bright morning, when the sun
rose powerfully in the sky,
this startling sentence was spoken to Penelope:
Penelope! "There will still be a horse"
that's what Odysseus said
and it's me. I'm leaving for ten years of study
and what will look accidental is my fate.
Your face and sitting send me far away,
and this look of yours is like
the frozen air created
among people in the room for a revered personality,
the look. The look propels me away from
the whole peaceful household
like a forest trap.

This bright morning when the sun is rising
more powerfully than usual
I'm going Penelope but you're
to stay put, Penelope.
Stay put Penelope.

There will still be a horse that will return me here
as it was—to send me far off from here.
"the inability to make fun of you and the wish to make fun of you
add up to a trip away" you say,
Odysseus from Penelope.
Odysseus to Penelope,
desertion.

"Penelope ve'Odisses," *Bat Ya'ana*, pp. 11–12

Gainsborough

Lilliputian courtesan. A spy of the spirit.
Your incomplete communiqué is dim.
Your body a sweet *afiqoman*.[14]
Reportedly—Gainsborough we'll call the girl.

Gainsborough cut from a yellow drape.
Bluer than blue with a brazen forehead.
Rendezvous empty bedchambers.
Maybe houses mean bedchambers?

The sap of your mind is in darkness,
stripping the skin of spring,
sunbeams weave braids in the soiree,

on the smoky rooftops a flash, roof honey is burning,

A red tile is a sandal to my feet.

Gainsborough, a velvet boy. The parlors are upon you Gainsborough.[15]
Influences from every side,
from every limb,
and perfection leans forward birthing itself
bowing to you.

Bat Ya'ana, p. 21

Data Processing 15

The influence of cinema on poetry is immense.
Crushed I was pressed into the stem of the anemone
as I went forth loftily to my adventures,
pained by light putting the autos to flight overhead
with the vapor of my mouth.
Unthinkingly we fell into the valley and silence
covered my head green and sweet.
A lovely scarecrow and a horseman, and me without a crumb
we were three hunters after a prey.
The task flowed around as a tiger emerged from the foliage.
So I was forced into slumber properly dressed.
And from on high the heaven took a picture of us.
With hair disheveled, face yellowed
                and finally aquiver. The fisherman showed up
at three. Three fastidious people
each was bent on his way we each gave a hand to a friend
sniffing in dismay. And the bells rang,
and wild mustard and cyclamen got theirs.

When I left the point of weakness,
everything shrank around. They continued on.
The ants went forth in a silly ship dance and noxious
                        weeds—
from their verge.
I fell into them and the tiger passed his time.
My heart went out to him, at four o'clock, consumed
with desire.
Like an amethyst, I was gathered breathlessly
with the final rays to the next day
glowing I was on the mountain peaks
with an unfinished whisper,
that the influence of poetry on the cinema is immense.

"Ibud netunim 15," *Bat Ya'ana*, pp. 58–59

Bird Song–Green Song
From *Shirat hatsiporim* (Bird Song, 1985)

I'm afraid to sing because of bird song
afraid to sing;
We should follow the fibers of sadness till the syrinx
in a complex, complete structure like the mysterious sphinx
the flaw and the wondrous—why must we hurt the bird
in order to reveal its secret, no need to grope in the dark—
to toss the song box into a curtain of light
deep in the bird's chest in a triangle which has a bulge at its base
and two thin membranes for tremolo and play in everlasting air;
We must follow after the nerve that produces the bird song
or—the joy;
Sadness is filled with song
it tightens and loosens like an electronic cable recording sounds
from a song box; by the music box,
I'm afraid to sing because of the bird's rich song,
in order to explain it—must we defile it?
The apparatus is hidden in nuclei and a wondrous brain, the system
      is reserved
in the hiding place of flesh and blood and melody,
notes in a tune;
The mission of song is for man and not for woman,
she listens
he sings without laying an egg.

Ten hours on a spring day the grove was flooded with green song
song green and ideal—the male bird sings and listens
the sign of his song is concealed like eternity in his head
he sings and listens to himself—
he deletes and changes and redoes according to his ear
all alone; the unblemished machine of song
it's wondrous to me.

"Shirat hatsiporim," Shirat hatsiporim, p. 39

It all adds up to

From *Qol: Shirim* (Voice: Poems, 1981–1986, 1987)

It all adds up to solar heaters and antennas
It all adds up to a black kerchief in the sky
It all adds up to sky
It all adds up to the Bat Yam horizon
It all adds up to Israeli ugliness
It all adds up to urban beauty
It all adds up to sunset
It all adds up to the color pink
It all adds up to pallor
It all adds up to transience
It all adds up to black on gray
It all adds up to lights going on and off
It all adds up to
It all adds up to evening
It all adds up to a sense of distance.

"Zeh sakh hakol," *Qol*, p. 27

[I talk about myself]

I talk about myself in generalizations
talk about myself in questions
talk about myself in visions.
What do I say about myself:
I see myself in fumbling questions
hanging in tall trees
on voice ladders
I talk about myself
high and low
tall and gentle
dull awkward voices
I talk about myself in the simplest of ways
I'm in the streets traveling on public lines
at regular times;
And sometimes I talk about herself
a woman star
a stormy young woman
When I speak about her enveloped in wind
when she's closed off in her speech
when she talks about herself
radiance enwraps her.

I keep talking about myself in generalizations
I talk about myself
in simple deeds and trifles
and lose my grasp of
how to talk about myself.

"Ani medabberet al atsmi," *Qol*, p. 31

Autumn Hands

The surprising and deceitful warmth of fall,
      it's short,
spreads out like a fashionable dress off the rack;
and the city's spindly nerves all around
mournful arching wires
on a background turning pink and dark gray black
disappearing at evening.
Flimsy chains close about its clamorous blue heart
and across from them the sea sinks into hiding
facing the sea of blue air above.

I compare myself to the flesh of an oyster trembling white
lying on the threshold-of-stone-basket-of-earth
in the eyes of a god of desire
coming to an end
between the hands of time

"Kapot zman-stav," *Qol*, p. 42

The Jasmine Bush

I've retraced my steps, to the jasmine bush;
conversing with it
I'm excited by the confidence
of white wrinkled little angels, now
fallen from on high, coming to rest in the
                              meager branches
like fine trays of fragrance,
with the brazenness of clear wind,
I've picked for myself a fragrant tray
every moment butterflies are born of it
with their wings beating at an eternal, constant
                              speed
they guard its precise nature

Jasmine is a wild shrub of the olive family
that grows mainly in the mountains.

"Sia<u>h</u> hayasmin," *Qol*, p. 49

[The angels seal our fate]

The angels seal our fate
is it really so
how the angels seal our fate
with a mighty flapping of wings
and when one's judgment is decreed,
does one feel the sunshine in retreat?

" Hamal'akhim ḥotmim et goralenu," *Qol*, p. 51

Sea

Joy of the sea;
The sea at rest and seduced;
The hidden nightmare of the sea
In the huge rainbow hand of the rock;
The soap smell rinsed off me,
Stormy on the depths and recoils
From the tide
Of claws crabs and scorpions,
Flotsam and jetsam appear and disappear
A tumbling mess of disjointed limbs;
Joy of the sea
And the sea's made a mockery of me
As it covers and uncovers
As it tosses out and takes back.

"Yam," *Qol*, p. 57

[My soul is estranged]

My soul is estranged
from poetry
throw it all away
the words the embellishments
The meters and the burdens
My soul is estranged from poetry time
And only with colors
without obligation
I want to observe the clean soft light
on everything
And to drown   in the fall

A necklace of hoopoes on a green lawn.

"Naq'a nafshi," *Qol*, p. 59

.

Data Processing 1
From *Retsef hashirim* (The Poems' Sequence, 1987)

Evening breeze in a nighttime coif
vegetable juices accustomed in their shawl
seal fairies dancing,
and the shoulders of slaves also darken,
South Africa folding toward the north—
the shape of a tongue, and feather clouds blown up to a bronze
balloon. The ringings of fruits sound out.
Emerald stones in the folds of her dress—
my girlfriend is a gorgeous fox, an arrayed
cat, the walls blush at her beauty.
It's clear to me that I'm no Darius with Persia crooked between my
    legs.
Quiet in the expected snow
turning green and a typhoon dizzies my cheeks
my eyes have flown off to Thailand,
the Prime Minister's eyebrows dance
like young boys, Markovitch rides on a centaur,
a whitish Messiah arrived
after the point in question.

"Ibud netunim 1," *Retsef,* p. 9

Night of the Fast

On a windowsill on a foul-smelling street in a
                    remote and crowded town,
its sole leader the Fast, rested the head of a
                                        girl
whose lips had been lovingly kissed
by the mouth of a slim-hipped neighbor boy
in a heat wave equally endured
by a fat woman on a footstool, hands folded
and by a day-dreaming yellow dog sitting beside
                            her, by a small doorway
on that same remote, crowded, foul-smelling street,
its sole leader the Fast.
And children skated on it freely
on black ice—a highway on the Fast day,
and the waste dough streamed over the sidewalks
gave off its own smell
along with the smell of clothing worn by people
seemingly content with their weariness
on a Fast day which served as their sole leader.
And the doorways, rectangular and square,
illuminated and open to the street, were filled
with dark heads, frozen without a single drop of
                                        melody.
Only a clamor arose and muted
the mutterings of a steadfast prayer,
and I walked through without scorn and only wanted
to sleep in the bosom of natural stone.

Yom Kippur Eve, 1973[16]

"Leil hatsom," *Retsef*, p. 130

[From the midst of morning]
From *Mizmorei Iyov* (The Hymns of Job, 1993)

1

From the midst of morning dozing moving shifting and a circular
     movement removing
and getting out of a single bed strewn with black and white cotton
     checks 7:00 A.M.
The cat's been meowing since 4:00 A.M. to be held and fed milk and an
     egg
why do I feed and hold her what sort of debt do I owe her what sort of
     need to go to her
a good point but impractical a white queen a bride
the secretary of an editorial board of high pedigree
shedding Persian hairs everywhere twisting and scratching I go about
     my toilette in preparation for a new morning.

There's no escaping from the body and a new day against our will
it's impossible to postpone it for even a second
because what what what, I've been and will be
and all of my will without lifting a finger all of my will
to see the eye of the storm of the luminous tyrannical order which
     rules me with its

                                                  careless popular
beauty
actually, a force of diligence which repels me with its vulgar habit or
     whatever they'll say
and already the feet are in the shoes
and I must wake my daughter from a sweet sticky sleep
with all the mulish force in me—
and now where to—and quickly *Tzena-Tzena-Tzena*[17]
says my neighbor in a Hungarian voice raspy as an old radio—don't
     stay
it's crowded but you'll still have to get in the long morning bus queue

Did I say I've weaned distant markets?
A baby girl who's been weaned—I've never been weaned and never will
     be weaned

from wanting to root my spirit in distant lands
to spread my wealth there on the beautiful and to learn the meaning of
    joy as on the Seine
                                            and the Arno
on the banks of the Ganges and the fountains of Rome
and I've wanted to forget the sands of Jerusalem because
I've not weaned distant markets of beauty riches and health
only the sawdust of silence in my footsteps the sawdust of my
    memories
the Hill of Markets I've climbed hurrying to the glorious ATM booth
to withdraw my money to gather strength and I reached into my hand
as if to ask for my hand I stretched my hand to the ATM
a checkered hand heavy with diamonds and sapphires
covered like an injured hand in a black handkerchief
like an injured hand in a black handkerchief and first red stains
I withdrew it from there

2

Suddenly I was stabbed from behind,
before me stood an angel, blacker than a speaking stone
and took me between its gnashing wings
like an elevator in an invisible skyscraper,
I flew I ascended with it, I descended with it, I was devoured,
vomited, excreted, and returned to myself with open eyes;
My loved ones leaned over me, and the more I smiled to them,
they wiped my nose and dried my tears, which certainly
did not flow from any place, but
the main thing is that we identified each other, that is,
we took photos together.
Suddenly I was stabbed again from behind, and an angel blacker than
    the one before,
blacker than a speaking stone, stood before me
and took me between its gnashing wings;
then it came to me that its bittersweet message
permeated my ears and I received a smooth shining
black color
we flew and ascended descended as if in an invisible
skyscraper elevator. And its dense message came to me

recorded and absorbed and immediately wrung into the form of a
    murky liquid
dribbling on me from my black pores
skin, that is
I was shiny as a rock and all the other angels sang along with me
in a raspy voice that completely infuriated me
how is it the angels are completely false
they've not practiced for thousands of years, the emissaries of divine
    thought
they've been petrified for years
ensconced deep in graves and veins,
in illustrated pages, albums, sculpted in marble in iron
and plywood, inlaid in glass
they got up and detached themselves from there rose up to sing with me
reading in chorus Come Come
and I did so and came and I obeyed the message
because those who will bring me to him they brought me to him.

"Mitokh haboqer," *Mizmorei Iyov*, pp. 7–10

Intermezzo

Truth is I was kidnapped.
Don't take me to the stony field
I pleaded
Don't plunk me in the bare stony field
On a hot day like this.
Craggy yellowish boulders, thorns, greenish desiccated shrubs,
Hills only hills and sky-y-y glorious of course
The sky doesn't interest me I screamed—
The Land,
My whole life on the Land—the concerns
Not the stubborn earth not a stony field
All of me is here with the people.
Look, you work blindly, understand!
I pleaded Don't! Don't! I screamed, a sailor
A crude seaman just like the one who tied me up to his boat and went
    off
Won't you pity my children, my lovely creatures?
Won't you pity my successful projects,
my wife and husband,
a slight silence, a murmur beating inside me
I'm aware my heart makes murmurs and I'm afraid

Truth is I was kidnapped
I also kidnapped, between me and myself
Everything was done with will and awareness
Unforced only by surprise
It was an upsetting surprise
Truth is I wished for him
Truth is I was just like him
Like the reflection of my death
In a crystal ball, waiting
Until I'd reach it with my whole self
And I'll be just like it at the end of my days maybe at the beginning
Maybe in mid-life—your time is over

We've sent you a sailors' lifeboat
For you to sail in the opposite direction—the heavenly chorus
Sings Come Come
And I've done this and came to realize
That they'd bring me to it
And they brought . . .

"Qeta beinayim,"*Mizmorei Iyov*, pp. 12–13

The Sixth Smile

And from the river came a boat
I was tied to it—
a boat of joys and pleasures
it was a boat of sorrows
and the poetry's power as a stack of rope
collected on the bottom
sailing up a dark tangled wild grove,
and five smiles floated along on my face:
a sovereign smile for the future
a gentle, forgiving smile for my past
a smile of triumph over present sorrows
a seductive smile readied for the meeting with him
and a smile for myself at sunset,
the sixth was the foolish smile—

The Corman family[18] smile,
that included five human smiles
the smiles that before death
sparkle for a good, broad field
a fruitful field with a colossal horizon
where their immortal home abides
an immortal home resplendent in beauty and repose
at a proper height for Heaven and for others

and they came back home in well-hammered coffins
from distant America
now smiling the sixth smile of a final summer.

"Haḥiyyukh hashishi," *Mizmorei Iyov*, p. 16

A Galilean Scene, I Must Point Out
Uncollected

A rectangular doorway to a hotel room
       I must point out
a suite of small rooms, one of eleven hundred like it
the Kinneret is a dull gray today.
The horizon is submerged in clouds, a steel blue
         I must point out,
I took it all in, at a certain time of day, let's say,
early noon, maybe morning
and later slowly slowly even a late hot
dry afternoon in winter
and I must point out, I wasn't by myself
but I took in the flat silvery surface
of the Kinneret which retained in her memory something
         I must point out:
the sweat of the young visionaries on her banks,
in fields as yet uncreated,
tears of all her drowning victims, the voices of pioneers
the slap of fisherman's oars, motorboats
shouts of pleasure and excitement
         I must point out,
of tourists, the calls of feasting pilgrims
it was all wrapped tight in her depths
         I must point out,
rinds and remains of meat and charcoal, breadcrumbs, empty wrappers
and the fish, I must point out
were wondrous and begrudging.
I was level with the gull's tilting,
         not by myself
in the rectangular doorway the sunshine is still blinding
from the room in the tiny hotel suite
an idea is flung out, a gull is mercilessly battered
         I must point out
that at the last moment the gull is lifted up in the saving retina of my
    glance

I must point out,
that in the margins of the shoreline
well marked and always endangered—depending on the season
on the look in her eyes and her will,
appeared boughs of bougainvillea and thick reeds,
dull green coots, decomposed blossoms,
smooth pier-like stones,
and the presence of palm trees was persuasive
for burial there
I must point out.

Ha'aretz, February 21, 1997

There Were Pecan Leaves

[a.]

There were pecan leaves a mere
   backdrop
pecan leaves were the backdrop
the late one that came later,
and before the backdrop of pecan leaves—
there were thousands of faces,
whose number owing to a passion for profusion
(like the apples of lovesick Shulamit)[19]
I can't state precisely.
Faces near faces far
faces close by faces at a distance
faces to arrive tomorrow faces of yesterday,
and we were all knotted together in some
uncommon presence, not so much
as comrades knotted together in a presence
let's say a pretty
piece of light familiar music
Clark and Hummel and Rimsky-Korsakoff and Bach
the Beatles and Gershwin.
Piano keys marched up and down
fat contrabass chords provoked with their
   low pitch,
and the trumpeter who so much resembled dark
   Father Frollo[20]
that the medieval church of Notre Dame instantly vaulted up,
   thanks to the gazelle,
the trumpeter dressed like a court musician in a place
managed to add to the act of knotting together
an effortful stain visible on my lip.

I'm striving
to keep on playing,
to keep going up,
and the train of faces is getting heavier already turning

into the pearliest of pearls.
The sun's already at a blunt angle past the meridian
leached, beams simple unpretentious:
just about 2 o'clock,
it's no problem to describe:
Luzit, the Valley of Elah, Agur
a stone structure a lofty lookout
a Turkish khan,
acacia trees in a marvelous yellow
with branches of olive and carob.
I want to turn back
to turn back
to the pure white pearls behind.
Not because I've overlooked a mouse,
there's no mouse
a chill wind has moved in to blow
the notes away,
so someone's scared
to hold them fast with his dead cell phone.

But we've not yet smelled the blood
(not the Maccabean blood)
we've played, merely played
and paid attention,
how the players struck into the air alongside us
with us (that's the point, with us)

[b.]

There'll be pecan leaves
pecan leaves about to be
at any moment a backdrop,
at any moment in the backdrop,
they've sat there their backs a mere backdrop,
Eliezer's agèd parents and he by their side
and they facing their house about to collapse—
about to collapse,
it's lasted dozens of years
like them and this has been the main topic.

Three men in a cascade of afternoon light[21]
and in the backdrop pecan leaves,
in their precise place they've been at rest
and silence silence
even if strength was imputed to it
and the silence has begotten
the smell of blood.

April 1997

Ha-aretz, June 13, 1997

Erez Biton

EREZ BITON, born in Algeria to Moroccan parents in 1942, moved to Morocco in childhood and then later to the new State of Israel in 1948. He has remained active in Israel's Moroccan community and, modernist though he is, continues to feel connected with Morocco's venerable Jewish tradition.

In Morocco the family lived in poverty in small villages in the south of the country, then emigrated to Israel, where they were assigned to the transit camp at Ra'anana. Soon they moved to the town of Lod (Lydda), where they lived in an abandoned Arab house. Conditions were difficult: Biton's father worked as a laborer and it was difficult to support the family of seven children. Without an adequate living, he was forced to work for the army cleaning latrines.

The children ran wild in the fields and orchards around Lod searching for pieces of copper and other "finds." One day, when Biton was ten years old, he came upon an old grenade. He did not know what it was and hit it with a hammer. The explosion cost his sight and his left hand. In 1953, after a rehabilitation of several months, he was sent to the School of the Blind in Jerusalem.

There Biton was given the name Erez and learned Oriental music, Israeli culture, many skills, and other schoolwork. He graduated high school in the Lifschitz Seminar in Jerusalem and earned a B.A. in Social Work from the Hebrew University of Jersualem. He then moved to Ashkelon where he was employed for seven years as a social worker at the local welfare agency. Later he moved to Tel Aviv and completed a Master's degree in Rehabilitative Psychology.

Biton was concerned for his parents who remained in Lod, so he acquired a neighborhood grocery store. When he completed his studies, he worked as a psychologist for the local council in Or Yehudah. Along with his professional work he began to write poetry. Soon after, he became involved in politics, was a leader of the Sephardi struggle, and wrote several journalistic columns in the newspaper *Ma'ariv*. His political endeavors were focused on "Tami," a party called "The Movement of Traditional Israel," and brought together several Sephardi factions, composed mostly of Moroccans, to lead the protests.

Since 1983 Biton has edited a journal called *Aperion* (Canopy) for literature, culture. and society. Elected in 1991 to the chairmanship of the Association of Hebrew Writers, he served to 1993. He ran unsuccessfully for the Knesset (Israeli Parliament). Currently Biton is working to organize international conferences of Mediterranean writers in the interest of peace.

Since 1970 Biton has published his poems in several venues. He was one of the poets in the collection *Four Poets* (1976), and published three other books: *Minha marocca'it* (Moroccan Gift, 1976), *Sefer ha-na'ana* (The Book of Mint, 1979), and *Tsippor bein yabashot* (A Bird Between Continents, 1990). A collection of his poems was translated into Arabic in 1991 and his works were awarded the significant Talpir and Prime Minister's Prizes.

Biton's wife, Rahel Calahora, is an architect; they live with their son and daughter in Ramat Hasharon.

Biton's poetry projects a number of salient themes: his traumatic experience of blindness when he was wounded in 1952; his life at the School for the Blind; his family background; relatives and neighborhood events; marriages and other celebrations; his sense of an equivocal identity and authenticity as an Israeli poet. Other themes are children, memories of Morocco, superstitions, women in domestic and social scenes, folklore, and music.

Much of Biton's work is graphic, memoiristic, folkloristic, with a gentleness and genuine atmosphere. The style tends to be multifaceted: colorful, passionate, often understated. Biton's sensitivity is palpable to the various personae he delineates in these poems, whether he is limning a relative, a drunkard, or a forlorn boy. As remarked above, the poet has lived in two disparate worlds: third-world Morocco and developing Israel. Though some of Biton's scenes may appear stereotypical, the poems project a strong sense of realism.

Other aspects of Biton's oeuvre are his artless presentation and the blend of spoken Arabic and Hebrew translations. His abiding rhymes and repetitions engender a charming musicality, and the spices, dishes, aromas, and traditions he calls on create portraits of a vital culture transmitted from one home to another and one generation to its successor.

Song of the Cane

From *Tsipor bein yabashot*
(A Bird Between Continents, 1990)

When the children cross the highway with me
I tell them,
I'm a gentle man,
the cane in my hand
is not for beating,
but when they leave me
in the twisting street,
I'm the only child left afraid of the cane.

"Shir hamaqel," *Tsipor,* p. 7

At the School for the Blind in Jerusalem

We were children at the School for the Blind in Jerusalem
hiding on our tiptoes
pressing our cheeks to the glass door
to hear your lyre's tune, Efraim Manofla.
Across the unfamiliar corridors
like murmuring songbirds
blinding the melody.
You promised great love symphonies,
what do you say now
when you squeeze out a penny
with the three strings of a broken mandolin
at the central bus station in Tel Aviv.

"Beveit ḥinukh ivrim birushalayim,"*Tsipor*, p. 10

Families in the School for the Blind in Jerusalem

We children in the School for the Blind in Jerusalem
grab seven kids in one
and say to him
you will be our father
and say to her
you will be our mother,
and they meet one another
body by body
to gather some warmth
in a game of togetherness.
And they make up families:
one boy's called: Daddy Shalom
one girl's called: Mommy Shoshana
another girl's called: Sister, my Sister Rachel
and another boy's called: Brother, my Brother Yossi.
That's how we made up families.
We children in the School for the Blind in Jerusalem.

"Mishpaḥot beveit ḥinukh ivrim birushalayim," *Tsipor*, p. 11

My Father Made a Wine Party for the Neighbors

On the wounded night
my father made a party for the neighbors
with all sorts of pastries.
While my mother
kept her eyes open for the ravens.
And the women neighbors on tiptoe
moved in and out to light candles

For Rabbi Meir the Miracle Maker
and for Rabbi Shimon Bar Yohai.
And I
tossed and turned all night
in a stupor
to strengthen my mother's eyes
to soothe my father's mind

And on their own the women neighbors
moved in and out
to keep up the life of the party
with frankincense and myrrh
till the dawn
sealed the last of the dark.

"Avi asa mishteh shekheinim beyayin," *Tsipor*, p. 12

My Uncle in His Yearnings

My uncle is like a transistor, tuned to the Land of Israel
and when he gets there year after year on hot days
he says, jokingly:
"I'll take some sun from here in a barrel
to sell sun cheaply
to the Jews there"
and when he arrived this year with coat over coat
to keep from maladies and store up yearnings
my uncle plans for a small plot on the Mount of Olives
for anointing oil, for hot days
how lovely my uncle is, how genial
eternally
on the Mount of Olives.

"Dodi bega'agu'av," *Tsipor,* p. 17

An Ode to Those Consumed by the Inner Splendor

Humbly I bow to the wonder of your wrinkled faces
You, dreamers of Jerusalem
to celebrate the miracle of the revival of your remembrance within me.
Your name sparkles in me like a rod which suddenly flowers.
Rabbi David Hasin and your sign is nine daughters
all of whom are raised into the tradition.[22] And you, Freha, the daughter
    of Yosef
you are wholly a bride with your veil
drumming the lines of the song
as in silver bracelets.
And you, Shlomo Gazlan
your song business at the fork in the road
balsam and cinnamon and all the best spices.
And I too will answer all of you with song
form the height of faith and from the summit of Senir.
From my lot and the pace of my life
to build a nest for you, a permanent home with me.

"Shir-shevah le'utei ziv hapanim," *Tsipor*, p. 20

Moroccan Wedding

1

If you've never seen a Moroccan wedding—
we've heard, we've heard,
blessed are your arched hands on the drums of the tamtam,
Sarah, daughter of Dodo,
from one end to the other of the village
Arab and Jew we'll come.
We've seen, we've seen
the latent power of arak, the endless skewers of roast dove
the layers of dates in seven kinds
at the entrance of the house
the pitchers of proud olives,
blessed are your arched hands on the drums of the tamtam, Sarah,
    daughter of Dodo
Arab and Jew we'll come.
Our heart slowly expands and our soul rejoices.

2

Ayyima (O Mama)
ten birds want to break out of my heart,
darling darling my soul, like a date from Biskra[23]
the sweetest of all,
your lips are two dates
from Biskra the sweetest of all
Ayyima
I bear the light of this evening as a burden of loss unconquerable
Ayyima
I feel like the earth two cubits beneath me
my darling darling of my soul
your neck like a slim wrist, like a forefinger
adorned with the cords of my heart.
It will be said again and again: since your wedding
                there's been none like yours.

3

Mama,
I too want a salad of cooked peeled pepper
seasoned with ten spices.
I too want a roll with a hardboiled egg, blended with lebzar and cumin.
Drum the tanbul:
Ta te te te te te
te te te te te te te te te
Naq te'ish (live long) Sheikh Hasen.
Come drink a glass of arak with me, Sheikh Hasen.
You didn't have to bring all these delicacies, Abu Muhammad, dear
     friend
and you, play the tanbul,
What's this, you all by yourself in the corner while we
enjoy your performance?

4

If you've never seen a Moroccan wedding,
if you've not heard Grandma Freha
trill the maqama[24] of passion in the ears of the bride and groom,
if you've not reclined on bright-colored cushions with your own two
     hands,
if you've not held a moist salad in your hands and bathed your mouth
     in the
                                        wine of Marrakesh,
if you've not sliced the bread with your own two hands,
if you've not breathed in the youthful clamor of our maidens,
if you've not been to a Moroccan wedding, here's your invitation
come join in
a heartfelt tumult
you've never felt before.

"Hatuna Morocca'it," Tsipor, pp. 33–34

On the Agadir Quake

That evening
the sky was blue with a core of gold,
the earth stood still in a silence of ambush,
those who remember say
the air was so sweet to breathe,
Tuesday evening it was.
How does it happen
    O Mama Mama
that respectable, rational people
will rise all at once groping shrieking in the dark,
how does it begin
    O Mama Mama
that a whole city will rise all at once
groping shrieking in the dark.
And later
    O Mama Mama
what does he think who contemplates
the ruins of his home
the loss of his dear ones
what is the first thing he'll do
that morning.
    O Mama Mama
that the morning would not come
and those who remember say
that evening
there was a sweet appetite for sleep
Tuesday evening it was
    O Mama Mama

"Al re'idat ha'adama beAgadir," *Tsipor,* p. 36

Hoarse Rababa

What are you seeking in me taste of another time
juice of a huge watermelon
sparkle of date pits
What are you all seeking in me hands for a game of five
I who went forth with a harp to coax the Furies
came back scorched.
In vain now
a tiny tamtam drum calls up in me thrilling fingers
In vain a summer sweetness beats eagerly on my eyeballs
two broken silences
now
my heart's dead to white bridal veils.
To the juice of a huge watermelon.
now
I'm a hoarse rababa[25] in a black breast.

"Rababa tseruda," *Tsipor*, p. 57

Uncle Yehuda Sharvit Between
Marrakesh and Dera

When my uncle got drunk,
he'd hang by his hands from the doorframes and the cottage walls.
He'd fall off his feet and gargle all the laughter and all the sorrow in
    him.
I knew of him that he was seen as shut up tight,
hidden in his drunkenness
saying wisdom within wisdom
truth within truth with the appearance of another "I."
Today, Uncle Yehuda is a name in a scroll
on the mouth of a corked bottle
between the roofbeams
there in the village of Lemhamed
between Marrakesh and Dera.

My aunt Sara
Sara the daughter of Dodo, ·
was you might say a champion tamtam drummer
When she drummed she turned the heart's trembling to joy
blended with the setting sun.
People went out in the field stood still:
"Sara daughter of Dodo declares a holiday
Sara daughter of Dodo declares a holiday."
Today, Aunt Sara is a name, in a scroll
on the mouth of a corked bottle
between the roofbeams,
there in the village Lemhamed between Marrakesh and Dera.
I who stand here now
stamp their name in silver and gold.

"Hadod Yehuda Sharvit bein Marrakesh v' Dera," *Tsipor*, pp. 59–60

Synopsis of a Conversation

What does it mean to be authentic,
to run in the middle of Dizengoff shrieking in Judeo-Moroccan:
"Ana men elmagrab ana men elmagrab"
(I'm from the Atlas Mountains, I'm from the Atlas Mountains).

What does it mean to be authentic,
to sit in Cafe Rowal in gaudy clothes (*agal* and *zarbiya*),
or to announce loudly: "My name isn't Zohar, I'm Zaish, I'm Zaish (a
    Moroccan name)."

And not this, and not that,
and in any case another tongue swells in your mouth until the gums
    explode,
and in any case beloved, discontinued odors are condemned
and I fall between the lingos
at a loss in the babble of voices.

"Taqtsir si<u>h</u>a," *Tsipor*, p. 61

The Odors Improved

What do you all want of me,
an arak taste and a pungent saffron smell,
I'm no longer that same kid,
lost among the legs playing pool
in Cafe Marco
in Lod.
Now, guys,
I'm learning to eat ice cream from a crystal
from a car that makes bird sounds
in the evening,
I'm learning to open doors
in antique music boxes.

Now
women who taste strawberry
teach me to sniff out Shakespeare bindings
from the seventeenth century
teach me to play with a Siamese cat
in a green salon,
guys.

"Tiqun harei<u>h</u>ot," *Tsipor*, p. *63*

With the Boys

Strike the thigh by hand
instantly you'll land
in the B'nai Melel.

That's what we speedy boys in the Quarter would say.
Now there stands over me Seido Lehevel—cross-eyed
cajoling me:
You were the fastest runner in the neighborhood,
I don't tell him his cross-eyedness is evident,
      even in his voice.
There are boys who've never known me,
who sneak up on me and put in my hand
a quivering bird,
but I'm not angry
a quivering bird is a living heart,
I let her go free living heart skyward.
Most of the boys like me
they tell adventures of walking on a high, wobbly fence
or throwing stones at a tree in the distance without missing,
and among the bigger boys are some who put coins in my hand.
When you grow up, my mother said to me, you'll be like Mr. Masood,
playing an oud, sitting, attracting a crowd
and making them happy.

"Im hayeladim," *Tsipor*, p. 71

At the Women's Feet

Who will redeem your barrenness Alala Isha, daughter of Masooda
a woman withered, square,
whose entire house is a bedroom
and one tree and an old husband
her entire life spices, pepper, cumin, gourd, lebzar,
her entire business cooking that's turned out well or cooking that's
    been burnt
I loved the way she'd describe prolific mothers:
They beget children seven at a time
like a litter of blind kittens
feeding them with straw and hiding them in the stubble.
My mother imposes her own view:
This isn't on your account Alala Isha, this is on account of your taking
an old husband.
I'm nine or ten
a boy who's given a handful of figs
and seated on a stool in the sunshine
at the feet of the women
and is forgotten
and I listen and don't listen and know the ways of women
and everyone who comes and goes in the B'nai Melel Quarter.
Alala Isha Alala Isha,
Now I'm going to betray to you the rumors
the children whispered behind your back:
Look at this woman in whose belly a child died,
and that the women would spit out at your heels: Phooey! *Allah yister*
    [God watch over us]

and they'd warn their children not to touch you.
I remember you Alala Isha
your gentle hand on my head forsaken on the stool in the sunshine.

"Lemargelot hanashim," Tsipor, p. 72

Raquel Chalfi

ISRAELI-BORN RAQUEL CHALFI spent her childhood on a kibbutz and in Tel Aviv. During her early teens she lived in Mexico, where her parents taught in Hebrew schools. Returning to Israel, she served in the Israel Defense Forces as a journalist. She studied English literature and philosophy at the Hebrew University of Jerusalem and was awarded a Master's degree. She is also a graduate of the American Film Institute in Hollywood, California.

Chalfi's family has an honored place in twentieth-century Hebrew literary and artistic history. Her father, Shimshon Chalfi, was known as a poet. His older brother was the renowned poet and actor Avraham Chalfi. Raquel's mother, Miriam (Baruch) Chalfi, is a sculptor and a poet.

While Raquel Chalfi studied at the Hebrew University, she tutored fellow students and also served as a producer and editor of Israel Radio broadcasts and worked as a director of documentary television films. She has continued to work in broadcasting, and has taught film at Tel Aviv University.

Chalfi has written plays and screenplays and has directed some independent films. Her writing and work in the media have won awards in Israel and abroad, but she is known mostly as a poet and has published six collections: *Underwater and Other Poems* (1975); *Free Fall* (1979); *Chameleon or the Principle of Uncertainty* (1986); *Matter* (1990); *Love of the Dragon* (1995), and *Stowaway* (1999). Her poems have been translated into English and other languages and have appeared in a number of journals and anthologies. In 1989 and in 1998, Chalfi's work was awarded the Prime Minister's Prize for Literature.

In her poetry, Chalfi strives to comprehend and absorb the world, its various phenomena and characteristics, larger and smaller, outer and inner. The poet approaches this awesome undertaking by way of sharp perception, passionate reflection, and extravagant imagination. Landscapes and images abound: the sea, a shore restaurant, stones, colors, the moon, the cosmos, quantum physics, the chaos, the light and the dark, asleep and awake. The settings are fairly familiar, but other scenes blend colorful and fantastic portraits: a strange submarine, a spaceship, a dragon's domain, a flying dream journey, an angel. A darker world also lurks below: monstrous beasts, wastelands, and boundless emptiness.

As to the real world, Chalfi presents a tremulous universe, an existence made of molecules, a dubious validity. Like "a blind mole running through a tunnel of hope," the world's populace is groping with obscure currents and contradictions. Fear, loss, and insecurity reign. The heart yearns for a bit of soulfulness, but like a child lost in a primeval forest, life is tenuous and forlorn.

Chalfi's poetry is expressive of sensuousness, passion, self-irony, a texture of relativity and tentativeness. The only true stability is one's own body and its rather thin skin. The self seeks a sanctuary, an "intra-earth existence," an "inner awakening." An echoing plea cries "make me grow," as if one cannot fully cope with the worldly experience.

In her quest for innovation and humaneness, Chalfi embraces a wide span of literary and cultural territory. She alludes to a long list of items, both classical and contemporary: the Bible, modern physics, Glenn Miller, the Beatles, Bach, Handel, Sleeping Beauty, Gregorian chant, *shiva*, the Odyssey, Alice in Wonderland, Bluebeard, and a whole gallery of UFOs and aliens.

Rich in irony, her works demonstrate a semiromantic mode bringing together oppositional phrases, not only light and dark, asleep and awake, but paleness and brilliance, real and fantastic, secure and fearful.

Another innovative feature of Chalfi's poetry is the pausal breaks in the graphic arrangement on the page. The breaks and spaces may give pause so that the reader can better digest the text, but the main purpose of this design is Chalfi's aspiration to shape each poem as a living, breathing organism.

Sounds at the Beach

From *Ziqit o eqron i-havada'ut* (Chameleon
or the Principle of Uncertainty, 1986)

In the foreground
a Glenn Miller record   sizzle
of steaks on the grill   electronic beeps
the click-clacks of an adding machine
I can't   I
can   a hot sandwich please
when I met him   when I met her
noise noise in the steak place

In the inner background
noise inside my head   a little
stirring within a stirring   wild cereal   and fears with
cinnamon   of a bit of a brown dream

In the back background
but up front   beyond the window pane
the rolled silence   the great song   of the round sea
over which the pen cannot prevail
and I cannot prevail
as it is for the other things
spherical

"Kolot leyad hayam," *Ziqit*, p. 19

What Tenderness There Is
From _Homer_ (Matter, 1990)

What tenderness there is in our body as it
slowly
abandons us,
unwilling to cause us pain
with a sudden blow.
Slowly   lustfully
like a semi-Sleeping Beauty
it weaves us small wrinkles
of light and wisdom—
not fissures of an earthquake—
an airy network of grooves of fear.
How generous of our body
not to change our face
all at once
not to break our bones
with one blow

No,   cautiously
like a pale moon beaming its brilliance upon us
it illumines us
in a network of grieving nerves
folding our skin at the corners
hardening our spine—
so we can stand all this

What beauty   what tenderness there is
in our body slowly betraying us
politely preparing us
telling us in a whisper
bit by bit   hour after hour
that it's   leaving

"Eizo adinut yesh," _Homer_, pp. 12–13

Quarrel

I have a quarrel with words.
I push them away   I don't
trust them   especially when they're   light
lacking
a kind of matter   a sort of warm body joining them with something
    else
stirring somewhere inside
the stomach's geology
a kind of intra-earth existence
a kind of murmuring layer
hurting not exactly in my stomach   not exactly in the earth
but somewhere beyond
and despite this   interlacing with myriads of arteries and veins
impalpable   and yet how very palpable
into the body
into the earth's body
this body of bulk upon which I swarm

And only when the words
plod after a kind of warm body like this which joins them
with these groping masses   wrestling with piles of muteness-scream
only then I
a blind agent among obscure currents   unclear matter
perplexed among different weights   trying to navigate
like a blind mole digging a tunnel of
hope
a stream of light dimly illumines the murk
between chaos
and chaos

"Riv," <u>Homer</u>, p. 20

When Your Brain Waves

When your brain waves join with ocean
waves
When the frenzy of thought dissolves into
the inhale-exhale of the great body
of this gigantic, sprawling beast,   the ocean
When your own tiny, frail eardrum absorbs the beat
        of the drums of the deep

Again I repeat: When your brain waves merge with
the waves of the sea-ea-ea-ea
When small geysers of electric activity in your brain
spray into   are swallowed into
the expanse of the breathing blue
of the Great Sea

When your own waters dissolve into the great waters
hugging the sea,   the udder of the earth,
drowning in the midst of Being

At a rare moment like this
I say again: In a minute-splinter as rare as this
I   (my stubborn brain)
know once again,   for a moment's duration,   a minute-splinter:
Yes
there's still a chance

"Keshegalei hamo'a<u>h</u>,"*Homer*, p. 35

Through Every Body

Passing through every
body
I come to you more
I pass through them
as if I'd gone through fire
Through them I strive to your body
as if I were a small flame
exposing itself to the storms
They'll rise in me, make me grow
I'll rise and strive toward you
shutting myself, seeing you like a distant breeze
that will blow in me once
and for all

"Derekh kol guf," _Homer,_ p. 38

Winter in Jerusalem

My sleeping bag fell apart
It vomits up hard paradox
after
paradox.   The flesh, surprised,
bristles for battle.
The glittering sword of cold
strikes
at soft essences
tames them into the lining of the brain

A barking cold demands
a heavy tax
stubbornly gnaws and gnaws.
All the coats of memories
are in disarray.
A foolish wind slaps my face
with imponderable contradictions

A stupid winter biting with its ravenous mouth
a furious winter striking at my eyes
a winter slashing insolence at my teeth
what a winter
in Jerusalem

"Horef birushalayim," *Homer*, p. 40

Primeval

I feel the primeval wastelands
the winds wailing again and again
the hostile eons
the earthquakes
the stubborn icebergs
the long winds
the dinosaurs
the dense stirring
the expansive emptiness
the incomprehensible melody
the twisting length of time

I see the sun
through it I hear
the eternal night

"Qadmoniyot," _Homer_, p. 54

Should I

From *Ahavat hadraqon* (Love of the Dragon, 1995)

Should I lift a small leg
over the hedge
and be flung into the world of intricate
forms like lattice which ancient artisans with
tangled beards had woven
with pure and simple patience?
Should I take flight on the sounds of the mad singer's
throaty voice   or feel in my belly
the roots of the old familiar mattress
on which I lie on my belly   almost in flight
but   firmly grounded?
Should I drown in the mire of imagined love
carved by my brain's hologramic
mechanisms   or sink into soil
that has no imaging   that has only
what exists?
Should I swing leisurely on the sculpted words
or look within myself for a hairsbreadth
of silence?

Should I give in   be in thrall to threads of sleep
which are turning into ropes?
Should I eat what comes by
like ice cream
and melt with it?

"Ha'im," *Ahavat hadraqon*, p. 8

Birthmark

I have a birthmark
no one can see

In quiet moments   when only
I and my body are alone in the room
I unveil it
gaze at it
stoop down to kiss it

One night   I was calling it by names
all through the night
but it did not come to me

it left me alone with my body pure
flying in a dream-journey to other bodies
rubbing against them   whispering whispers in their skin
only to teach them the meaning of
a birthmark

All through the night I called it by names

At dawn it came back to me
loyal
and sat at the foot of the bed

As soon as my body was opened
it pounced on it with a warm, rough tongue

Sometimes I wish it would never come back
but later
I see that's how things are

"Ketem mileida," *Ahavat hadraqon*, p. 14

Look   Look the Dragon's Turning

Look   look the dragon's turning
his teeth
Look   his serpent-tail's turning into
a golden fleece
don't let him get near me
even if he turns into
an angel
burning
No   don't let him get near me
and lick me like a sheep   lick
as he grazes in meadows   for who
will make me lie down in the meadow
as a fiery dragon comes near me
bleating in skin not his own
for who will rescue my meager skin
when his cruelty turns into
a multitude of golden curls
don't let him turn like
a sword
into an angel
for look   look he's getting near
me
for who will rescue my meager innards
as his eyes turn into
flaming gold
Look
Look he's inside me
No   Don't

"Hineh   Hineh hadrakon hofekh," *Ahavat hadraqon*, p. 15

Nothing

Nothing compares with life itself

The poem   its tail between its legs   flees in the face of
disease   in the face of holding on furiously by a
nail   to a fragment of life
the picture on the wall breaks down to clouds of
                                        molecules and flies off
in every direction   beyond the wall behind which
someone's already spent a week vomiting up his life   the music
sounds like the howling of a torn cat   when it
booms from a radio in an internal medicine ward

Come now, write a good singable song   patients in white robes pull at
        the hem
of my dress as I help a man   step   by   step   to walk
and I see around me a huge black empty bowl
I'm poured into its bottom   trying
to climb its slippery sides from within
trying to climb
trying like
like   like   like
oy   oy   oy
forget pretense
forget high jinks
to hell with words

                    and writing—

is a spasmodic race to a dream of
freedom
dreamt by a beast
taken prey

"Shum davar," *Ahavat hadraqon*, p. 54

Submarine Blues

Submarine   Submarine   don't be so
sad   Don't be so low
Listen   It's not that bad
True   you've really gone way down
you   who were yellow and cute
but maybe you'll begin absorbing the fact:
here, too, you can survive until the oxygen's
run out   and this won't happen so fast.
So what if you're sunk?
Meanwhile why not send some
signals to the glowfish?   Look how
he makes light for himself in this deep dark.
Let him wink at you what's wrong   let yourself be taken in a bit.
Or meanwhile why not use
the periscope? Maybe you'll see there in the distance far above
some forgotten   little   beach
And then you'll hum to yourself   below
some dry   little tune?
And in the role of a plundered sub with kisses and a tinge of light
    and with
a hummable landlubber-tune   won't you be for me once more
a dashing rosy sub?
Submarine   so help me   stop
being this way!   So what if you're lost there
stuck?

"Tsolelet Blues," Ahavat hadraqon, p. 59

Stone

Cast into my body
like a fossil into
a primeval stone.
A hard hardness everywhere
and a finger that will strike this stubborn rock that's me
will produce from it a muffled sound
as if strata on strata of eons
had petrified its heart
and the words and the words come forth in slow procession
words of stone
so remote
from this quivering which is mute and only
its voice tears
like the voice of a primeval beast in primeval dark

words have remained for me broken poles to lean on
and the voices where are they
and fear alone

and this crude beast-of-life
a shrunken knot inside me
well cast into a world of total stone
and concealed in me like an ancient mollusk
that has hardened
and I am hard   greater than it
I
I am the stone

"Even," *Ahavat hadraqon*, p. 60

I've Come Back to Your Bosom   Great Sea

I've come back to your bosom
Great sea
Once again   after
an exile of continents
from myself

I've come back to your bosom
Great Sea

Sea
Goddess   the Deep
Monster-goddess
Sea   there   there
Sea   coming near
Sea inviting you to drown

Sea-heaven   there
Sea gaping wide
Yawn
Deepening
Swallowing   maw
Sea
Deep

Deep-Monster-
Goddess

Tiamat

"H̲azarti el h̲eikekh, hayam," *Ahavat hadraqon*, p. 61

Mordechai Geldman

MORDECHAI GELDMAN was born at Munich, Germany, in 1946 and emigrated to Israel in 1949. He has earned a B.A. degree in general literature as well as a Master's degree in Clinical Psychology, and practices as a psychotherapist in Tel Aviv.

After the Second World War Geldman's parents moved from Poland to Germany. During the Holocaust Geldman's father had seen his first family murdered; his mother hid in a village. Later his parents found each other, and his father traded in gold and silver in the black market. When the family moved to Munich, the Allied Powers gave them a room in a Nazi's house. After the family settled in Tel Aviv, Geldman's father established a small factory for plastics. When it failed, he opened a grocery, which brought a respectable living, and ultimately turned to selling furniture. His mother loved literature, was accomplished in Polish and Russian literature, and later became familiar with Israeli literature.

Geldman attended Orthodox schools, but at the age of sixteen he ceased to be Orthodox. At the same time he published his first poem in a youth newspaper. At seventeen he became interested in psychology and went on to study at Bar Ilan University. He showed his poems to Yona Wollach and published some of his poems in the journal *Akhshav* (Now).

To date, Geldman has published eight collections of poetry. He has also published a professional book entitled *Psychoanalytic Criticism* and *Dark Mirror,* a collection of essays on psychoanalysis, art, and literature. Over the years he was awarded several prizes: the Chomsky Prize for Poetry, and the prestigious Brenner Prize and the Prime Minister's Prize in 1998.

Many of Mordechai Geldman's poems reflect the themes of an analytical quest: inner struggles, the power of the poet, travels, distance, freedom, absence, loneliness, sensuality, and self-identity. He often contends with his own future—how to grow, be, work; he "prefers a poet," wants to live in his own nature, in perfect freedom, unfettered, not in "the windows of a prison." Geldman eschews fixed regulations—he calls them "word" or "verbal orders," created by others. He is not interested in power; he lives "outside of power," "in the depths," he declares.

In the poem entitled "Eyeing," the eye is all-seeing: it looks deeper into margins of consciousness, penetrates the world, brings tranquillity, discovers mysteries, creates the world. The eye as a metaphor may well be the poet himself as a detached function, the source of consciousness and of tears, an omniscient viewer of life that knows it can see only what it creates or reveals.

Despite the poet's worldliness and perceptiveness, there are different aspects of his life: its loneliness, its wanderlust, its sensuality, its neediness, and "gracious flesh and monastic austerity." The poetry portrays the "sacred laws of cities, roads, tramps," constant moving, vague goals, "strangeness." Each condition has its challenges and satisfactions.

Geldman embraces many fields and cultures. His reach is perhaps not surprising for a psychoanalyst confronted professionally and temperamentally with the inner as well as outer manifestations of human experience. Readers come away with a impression of the poet as *uomo universale*, a genuinely Renaissance personality, conversant with Greek mythology, world and Jewish history, Chinese culture, the fine arts, flora and fauna, the expanses of the literary imagination.

Dual images, "oppositions," abound in Geldman's poems. He is never distant from awareness of ambivalence and ambiguity in himself and in his surroundings or from recognition of the tangled nature of the human psyche. One supposes him to place great value on freedom from overwhelming emotion and to prefer a meditative perspective. His esthetic achievement calls to mind Cassirer's notion of art as "a discovery of reality" and a "revelation of [the] inexhaustibility of the aspects of things." The poetry substantiates Cassirer's view that "our aesthetic perception exhibits a much greater variety and belongs to a much more complex order than our ordinary sense perception."[27]

Non-Poem Non-Religious (Comparative)
From *66–83* (1983)

I can't identify the girl who's with me
but she's part of this journey
just as this journey is I, it's a journey of I
to not-I, a conscious journey to a no-words sea
a conscious journey that's a glowing arrow, a white ship,
from collective consciousness
to an unconscious sea
and this unidentified girl, this unconscious girl
this sea girl
travels with me in a taxi through the streets of a great city
the streets of a whole city, over ruins of Muslim, Christian and
Jewish shrines
and I tell her these are the most beautiful of ruins
because they're coastal cities, at the gates of God, at the gates of the
    ocean,
at the gates of the un-known
and the holiness of the places is only a justified fear
of the infinite chaos and infinite law
separating the concept of the divine from the concept of the human
and the prayer of these places is only a lament
that I don't identify you, I don't see you,
the girl that's with me.

"Lo-shir Lo-dati (Mishva'ati)," *66–83*, p. 61

Evening in Verona
From *Milano* (1988)

Evening in Verona only the living dine
on pinkish flowered tablecloths

Evening in Verona is an intoxicating blend
like the blue of an evening cleansed by the rain
to contain castles, thoughts and bridges
and the chatter of guys by a motorcycle

Evening in Verona only the living dine
on pinkish flowered tablecloths

The waiter passing by scowls
at me and other diners
the waiter passing by despises the diners
for reasons easily guessed

Evening in Verona only the living dine
on pinkish flowered tablecloths
they serve the magic of the moment
among dark castles on an island of light

It's easy to guess his contempt for the diners
is relief from his self contempt,
Solo, he asked when I entered
Solo, I replied, *molto solo,*
am I playing now?

Evening in Verona the wine is burning
on the pinkish flowered tablecloths
the waiter passing by lifts the lobsters
in the air that the rain has cleansed

"Erev beverona," *Milano,* pp. 31–32

Apollo 2

From _Halon_ (Window, 1989)

A golden lion on the basketball court
sucking cola with a white straw
a sweet stream of sweat from his armpit
to a wet stain on his shorts
a ball at his feet, his friends steaming
sun at the south of the court
a blinding roundness rising.
They said: "Dumb as a doorknob,
tossed out of school onto the street"
But snubbing their student mind
he quit to get ready for Apollo—
he flexed his muscles in burning garages
half-naked among tires and engines
anointed with grease
honey and sun blended in him
to flesh, whose wisdom is more ancient and complex
than the wisest of his teachers
honey and sun blended in him
to solid gold.

"Apollo 2," _Halon_, p. 25

Lone Ranger

I'm a lone ranger
in deserts of inner and outer cities
bound to sacred laws of gravity, wandering
tonight in labyrinth cities
smoky, steamy roads
lit yellow yellowing every color
of the space-age Luna Park
I flow in an impassive game of autos
which reveals the soulfulness of its players only in moments of accident
stopping for a beer in empty joints
transporting tramps to a vague, invented goal
devoted to my strangeness, belonging by sight

I'm a lone ranger
who last night snuck into the emptiness of your isolation
joyful in your warm, gracious flesh;
I don't imagine you other than as you are—
a girl of air in a land of titans
and your ability to spread out velvet
turned the motion into cloud riding
offering the monastic austerity an oceanic moment
doubly isolating tonight

In the morning I was afraid, you'll disappear, turn into
a pile of velvet, a wave of softness
from you to me might terminate

you in particular
me in particular

I'm a lone ranger.

"Parash boded," _Halon_, p. 27

Absence

The emptiness of shadow
the wasteland that reigns in her absence
her exit without slamming the door
when you read a book or fixed something
she slid from your life to another land
on hidden ice, a distance of stars.
It could be said that I'm in a desert in another galaxy
that the sky in this place is transparent iodine
and its silence hints at an ancient sea
of gelled lava in some antipodal region
but the simile's solemnity amounts to nothing.

Summer's outside
boys burning bronze
singing while painting the neighbor's apartment
boys burning bronze, their narrow hips
return from the beach with glass dust on their feet
and hold onto girls who cover themselves with colorful kaffiyehs
carrying fruit and dairy foods in woven baskets
their bodies shine cold as water and shadow
nice for the boys, the most bronze, the most burning.
Some children have fishing rods, others have a white ball
a small girl passes by on a green bicycle
on a street of ugly smoking buses
carrying people with summer links to their world
from one place to another more desirable,
beeping vacation beyond the window, at the distance of a hand, the
    distance of stars the distance that your heart has sailed away
and from here that distance is a function of the meaning of absence
and the season does not set the level of pain
but its color
—transparent endless iodine.

"He'ader," <u>Halon</u>, pp. 32–33

Kilimanjaro

I was dumbfounded when Kilimanjaro appeared
in my rotten, muddled head, exposed
on the pillow like an object, ruined by the evening
and I didn't remember it's a mountain
and didn't remember if it's Kilimanjaro or Kilimanjaro
but through the layers of cloud, through the blankets of whirling snow
suddenly appeared Kilimanjaro or Kilimanjaro, sparkling in black ice
bald, grass-raging, tree-frozen, bereft
of sun memories and a medley of fantail birds' variegation, it forgot
the pink flow of pastels flowering cherry, almond and plum
and below it gaping valleys, brimming springs, herds of deer, noble
    monkeys
with the gentlest movement, to the brink of petrifaction.

A mountain, I thought, reigns over its scenery
much as the brain over the emotions
like gods dominating the plain, an eternal mount,
a mountain immutable in the transitory, its secret the clouds
a mirror mountain, a mountain that may not be a mountain
a fantasy of brain frost in the head
on the pillow, on the flowered sheet, on the mattress
on the bed at eight P.M.—when it is unbearable.

Warm girls and a black singer were singing:
Kilimanjaro, Kilimanjaro, Kilimanjaro, marvelous and summery.

"Kilimanjaro," *Halon*, p. 42

Kaddish

To my father

Yitgadal veyitqadash God's Name be exalted and revered
who impelled you to wander from your Polish childhood to Kiryat
    Shaul

And so, with partial comprehension and full pain
illumined at times in snatches of joy
you set out gratis in a satanic train, you turned on a mysterious
    carousel
to the flowerbed of the long sleep

Did he know beauty, did he know the repose of reason?

By the sweat of your brow you had bread, we all ate bread
of his palms that I feared as a child
his beautiful palms my mother loved
mummified in memory, absorbed by dust
Yitgadal veyitqadash God's Name be exalted and revered

Who tore his eyes wide open to see
his daughter and wife and all the others, like the multitude of stars in
    the sky
considered trash of the world, murdered for cleansing, like ugly insects
in Europe, on the planet Earth that God created by His will
Yitgadal, yitgadal

And he built another house, in Palestine, in the Land of Yisroel of the
    siddur
with masses of other stubborn wanderers
by the blue sea, by the desert, near Jerusalem

And he saw his children grow, shut into worlds
devoted to concerns that to him were like voices from outer space
hurting, struggling, sometimes losing the way, sinking and floating
ever changing forms, again and again born

And he saw the trees growing on his street
and the wonder of television
the miracle of the visit in space
and the new wars, the wars, the wars
God—and at long last—"peace"
Yitgadal veyitqadash God's Name be exalted and revered

And what did you think of all this business?

That all will pass, it only takes patience?
—All will pass, it only takes patience
Yitgadal veyitqadash God's Name be exalted and revered
in the world that God created by His will.

"Kaddish," <u>H</u>alon, pp. 61–62

A Poet

From *Ayin* (Eye, 1993)

He preferred a poet
he preferred a poet over a journalist, a physician, a politician, etc.,
verbal orders given in advance, inset, created by others,
threatened him like the windows of a prison—
he tried to choose, to select
he pursued verbal orders that would suit
his nature as if his nature had preceded
the word orders or as if his nature were to be created
from more appropriate word orders
as if his nature were his future
and not a product of the patterns of his past
as if his nature were embodied in perfect freedom.

He preferred a poet
he preferred a poet over a journalist, a politician, etc.,
for he was outside the circle of power
for he was outside the structure of order—
words did not comprise him, subsume him or constrain him,
in the backyards of the word
in the filthy suburbs of the word
the strange and foreign suited him
even when surrounded by love, friendship and the portents of power.

He preferred a poet
for he sought to envision the word from behind it
for he sought the margins of the word and its opposites
he preferred a place that preceded power, a place in the depths of the
    mind
not a river but sources of a river
not a mountain but the valley from which the mountain had burst forth
not being but absence
from which innumerable beings have burst forth
not power, but a source of power.

"Meshorer," *Ayin*, pp. 46–47

Eyeing

The eye within the eye,
the eye origin and source of seeing
of the whole inventory outside her own existence,
the eye origin and source of weeping
which shone in her suddenly, to her surprise,
the eye pecking at the world
like a chicken at a heap of seeds
like an automaton chicken, foolish and nervous,
the eye which conceals the world
beyond the screen of eyelids
in the shattering gloom of a shameful inwardness,
the eye aided by eyeglasses
or preferring inferior sight,
the eye which creates the world
which sees what it shows
and admires the sights and her seeing,
the eye weeping over the nothingness
the eye weeping over a nameless want
the eye weeping for secret reasons
reasons known to herself alone,
the eye bewailing a pain thrust
ever deeper into the margins of consciousness,
the eye suddenly bewailing her bitter private knowing
like a bearer of bad tidings
to the ego bastioned in bright tranquillity
remote from passion and its objects,
remote from passion and its sorrow,
the eye time renders sightless,
the eye hungering now for a splendid view
(the base of five high peaks)
or at least, a postcard, a revelation, a news report,
the eye whose twin is symmetrical
and sometimes sees a poem.

"Iyyun," *Ayin*, p. 52

Bomb

Suddenly without warning or alarm
a long piercing whistle was heard
and in its wake came a bomb
which fell on my house with a deafening roar
and bestowed private spaces on the public space.

In the ensuing silence and the settling of dust
I saw that I'd been left bereft of possessions and family;
on my wrist a black Seiko watch
in my pocket a wallet with a credit card
on my body light clothing suitable for early summer in our country.

I poked about in the ruins
and found a few photos of the neighbors' soccer player athlete son
a girl's underwear printed with strawberries,
a cantorial recording, dishes filled with dust,
a tiny dog squashed flat, looking like a sock;
through the tears that welled up in my eyes
I saw that the whole city had been laid waste.

Anguished yet agile
I went looking for an empty field.
I said: this is the time of the field—
sit in the field and listen to the wind—
from every direction the wind blows
and no walls block the wind
and the field murmurs with the wind
and gives the homeless a heart and a place.

And in the blue star-spangled nights
you'll sleep in rustling groves
and you'll discover deep within your dream
what it was at which you launched a barrage of such deadly force
and was it a logical or lawful cause.

"Petsatsa," *Ayin*, p. 58

Porno 8

Torn from a real biography
torn even from her name
(always call her Lola, Lily, Lulu, or Lolita)
a night bride is she, a bridal night,
her audience she'll wrap in dark veils
in the dream night of the screening
in the starry night in which she'll star
in the night lit by the whiteness of her flesh—
she erases every biography,
she blots out every name.

What's left is only her body
what's allowed is only her body
her body shimmering from the covers of its secret,
her body made of light and remembrance
her body shared with all in need
like the loving kindness of the Mother in dimlit churches
her body shining forth in the night of screening
like a star for which imaginary spaceships set their course,
or like a truth uncovered from its blinding veils,
like a revelation,
like truth in its nakedness, like the nakedness of truth
like a truth about the uses of illusion.

Beyond the dazzling covers
beyond the darkness of the traitorous garb
in sexy flowered underwear
youth is exposed like her nude body;
In the space between her body and the eye of the observer
in the space between a memento of light and her real body
rise the fountains of desire.

"Porno 8," *Ayin*, pp. 100–101

Hymn: Porno 12

O naked queen
spreading across the huge billboards
advertising the froth of the moment—
we offer you our kingdom.
O goddess of eternal spring,
goddess of lustful orifices,
goddess of the joy of copulation and embrace,
goddess of the wave, the seashell, the flying fish,
we pray you, give us the hour of darkness,
we pray you, give us the moment of the kiss and the bite,
we pray you, give us beautiful bodies—
a young man his skin gleaming on muscles,
a young man, a hollow model of youth,
a young man freed of excess knowledge
and all of him blind loveliness
and all of him alive to the games of youth,
and a young woman her innards clean
and a young woman her innards pure
without memory or guts or blood,
but with honey and olive oil to lubricate
the motion of cocks in their lust
the movement that abhors procreation of man
and all her accoutrements agape
and delight tremulous as a momentary froth.
We pray you, night goddess of openings
we pray you, goddess of seas
give us the hour of deep night
when whores in the millions go forth to their whoring
scorned and bold rich and poor
and all of them beautiful as photos of models
and male whores join them
boys and lads penetrating and penetrated
who parade like shadows along curves and parks
bearing the hungry a chance for love
niches of hope at a reasonable price,

small strips of youthful memory,
vague, worn facsimiles
of a youthful embrace that promised eternal love,
an embrace that made you real
as if you were a bird, a star, or even a paragon,
or a fragment of remembered love
in the twilight before sleep
with the first love
remembered pale as milk and a blank page;
and as if renouncing an understanding
provident of sense and meaning
for the existence that has chosen lonely wandering
in a misleading maze of its possibilities,
the existence turning into galactic expanses;
and as if in the end choosing darkness.

O Venus, Madonna of genetic perfection,
now when our body's dwindling
give us pure physicality,
give us delight of orifices
when the great entrance swings open on our body,
and on the blue glory of the evening

and on the cursed and the blessed
and on the saints and the sinners
and on my seeing eyes and on the sights—
O Venus, give us froth at a bargain price.

"Himnon: Porno 12," *Ayin*, pp. 109–11
Translated with the author

Ficus Bonsai

From *Sefer She'al* (The Book of Ask, 1997)

He arrived without suitcases
since suitcases were unseen at his arrival
until I realized he dwells in my rooms
my life had become unusually bizarre—
Objects were displaced
Food left in pots was eaten up
Books I hadn't intended to read were found open on the sofa
One night the water in the toilet flushed
with a noise that tore me from my dreams
and I knew with certainty it wasn't I who'd use the bathroom
I was lying in my bed on the orthopedic mattress

These peculiarities and many others
seemed the tricks of an unseen spirit
but then to my great astonishment he
revealed his face

He chose to do so when I returned home
while listening to a river's roar
and to the birds singing on its banks
recorded for the well-being of city-dwellers
by a friendly American company—
he stood before me slightly embarrassed
his hands in a flower gesture
and above the orange colored monk's robe
raised his bold and boyish head
peeping at me with eyes of a frightened deer

Since he spoke Japanese
we couldn't discuss the way he'd invaded my home and his cause
but my deep friendliness to Buddhism
did not allow my heart to expel him
And I've permitted him to stay
as a spiritual mute friend
until he chooses to leave

But his silence did not eliminate his expressions
and surprisingly enough he had opinions on most of my doings
which he expressed with smiles that should be dubbed post-Buddhist
If they are to be seen as successors of the famous Buddhist smile of the
Buddha himself

He smiled at my exaggerated attention to my clothes
He smiled at my exaggerated interest in CNN
He smiled at my addiction to broadcasts of boxing matches
He smiled at my nervousness about my fame in the media as a poet
He smiled at my inclination to be sexually promiscuous
He smiled at my repeated disappointments in love
He smiled at my habit of escaping into sleep
He smiled at my fears of AIDS and other illnesses
and there were more reasons for more smiles;
He always sat aslant my gaze, never confronting it,
and sent his smiles in perfect timing

He even seemed to take a liking to me
and sometimes, when he didn't sleep on the windowsill or in the living
    room
He slept in my bed, naked clean and smooth as a girl
shrinking his body at the bed's edge
not to disturb my rest and dreams
and gradually I came to like him too—
Since he was a silent smiler
We avoided any disturbing misunderstandings
that follow long clarifying discussions
and I could imagine his purpose in accordance with my perspective

His smiles I thought were meant to sweeten my days
but also to detach all my attachments
he had a kind of spicy theory
that ridiculed any attachment to anything
beyond my attachments, he seemed to think,
there's a hidden question
the question I fear, the question I have to ask
the question I have to calm down with an answer

A kind of supreme *Ko'an*[28]
that will beat all firm answers
and all the dubious questions
among which I was dashing like a blind mole

Summing up the monk as a subversive and smiling question mark
or as a kind of Archimedes point from which
my being will be diverted from its track
did not excite me at all
and I preferred to seduce him
into the common passions of our society—
I hoped he'd give up his smiles gradually
and enjoy with me the pleasant nonsense which surrounded my being
various kinds of sorrow and worry included and I saw signs of such a
    conversion
since he started using one of my after-shaves

But before that battle of influences was resolved
He chose to vanish back to whence he came
leaving behind him a cloud of sorrow
since meanwhile I'd gotten used to his orange presence
and to the pure and delicate spirit that moved him
even when I indulged in the roughest energies

Many days I'll still be longing
for the evenings we sank into meditation
confronting each other with closed eyes
and between us blooms the Ficus Bonsai,
half tree, half picture, a contradiction of all measures

"Ficus bonsai," *Sefer She'al*, pp. 26–29
Translated with the author.

Ya'ir Hurvitz

BORN AT TEL AVIV in 1941, the late Ya'ir Hurvitz grew up during the years of the British Mandate and the early years of Israeli statehood. With his father's death in 1949, his mother became distraught; soon she and Ya'ir suffered a severe estrangement from each other. He led the life of an urchin and at school was viewed as a strange child. Victimized by degrading nicknames, he was mostly lonely and forlorn.

Hurvitz wrote his first poem at fourteen, and later, at sixteen, he met Natan Alterman. This was Hurvitz's definitive turnabout. He asked Alterman to look at his poems and Alterman became a source of encouragement. From then on Hurvitz was a familiar face on the Tel Aviv cafe circuit, especially the popular Kasit (Coral) and Vered (Rose) cafes. After publishing several poems in the late 1950s and early 1960s, Hurvitz worked in earnest to polish his oeuvre. His success was acknowledged, with eight collections from 1961 to 1976. During the next eleven years he was able to create six more collections, several of them published by the prestigious journal *Siman Qri'a* (Exclamation Point).

▧ The sixties, seventies, and early eighties witnessed a revolution not only in Israeli poetry, but also in Israeli politics (the aftermath of Israel's triumph in the June 1967 war and the costlier victory of the Yom Kippur War of 1973–74, the Likud government coalitions in 1977 and the 1980s). Israel was also affected by dual American revolutions (the civil rights struggle and the war in Vietnam) and a revolution in music (Rock and Roll and the Beatles). With the Beatles, the youth of the world embraced a new, original music sound. In Israel, the poetry of these decades reflected a new way of seeing and creating poems.

Hurvitz was at the forefront of this revolution. Others speedily joined: Meir Wieseltier, Dan Tselka, Gabriel Moked, Mordechai Geldman, and foremost, Yona Wollach. They called themselves "The Youngest of the Young."

Hurvitz's poems encompass large and various vistas. New landscapes, a sense of renewal, the "fabric of the sky," "a sea of light." These vivid images are mostly romantic: rustic impulses, adventures, inner conversation, secret faces, virgin sands, a feeling of primeval, bohemian existence, a golden glow of vitality, and "the beautiful years.

At the same time, another face portrays desolation, forlornness, colorless scenery, pictures without features, the light's shadow, darkness, shrunken distance, aging, and conspiracy. The poems in *Narcissi for the Dunghill Kingdom* (1972) are especially focused on this gloom and doom atmosphere.

The contrast captures the canvas of a dualistic condition that insists that life and death, however oppositional, are nonetheless compatible. Oxymorons and melancholy reign: "surging depths," "the heart's sorrow," "the serene tumult of beauty," "the eye darkness," "a sorrow festival," "The Book of Ills," and "Sickness Square"—all these epithets project a sense of dejection and despair. It might be that Hurvitz was reexperiencing parts of his childhood, or he might have been creating a new aesthetic, a deeply romantic poesy that parallels Baudelaire's Flowers of Evil, an artistic effort based on sarcasm, ambiguity, and irony.

Hurvitz also might have wanted to change the world, to heal its strife. He speaks about a "gentle voice" and a mystic speech housed in a mythical Temple where we can be healed by holy rites that cleanse our sins and wash away our misery. There will be festive joy, birds of delight, a place of sustenance and pleasure, a Shangri-la, a utopia powered by poetic fervor.

Hurvitz, born with a heart defect, died in July 1988, in Brussels where he had gone to seek medical care.

Word to Word

From *Narqisim l'malkhut madmena*
(Narcissi for the Dunghill Kingdom, 1972)

The gentle voice of the dead echoes with the voice of the living
just when the worm wanders from corpse to corpse
feeding splinters of flame.
Maybe then there's a weepvoice moving in the surgent depths.

If sewerdom is lacking in narcissus
come we'll set word to word for clamor
to silence the voice of the dead.

There's dust on the skeletal shoulders.
Let the worm wandering the flesh give answer.

"Davar el davar," *Narqisim*, p. 7

His Body Smites Love

As he went along he sought a place of sustenance a place of pleasures
and his body answered him with griefs and he became
one of the sun-blinded moon-watchers in great houses
gatherers of flowers in soft light. And his emblem

was silence
like a weighty fear,
like a house all window
with bitter waters hard as rock.

His body smites love as if it were a legacy,
it goes on encircling him like the sun.

And his emblem was silence.
He'd soar from radiant heights like a soft-plumed bird, like an ear
dropping into the depths listening in waters of delight, he'd come
like a bird of delight from watery heights.

Hear him, hear one.

"Makeh gufo ahava," *Narqisim*, p. 14

The Life and Death of Men

Thirty years maybe sixty
life and death
impose on the days of men.
Blessèd are those scattered with the sky
and with the wind calling them by the names of rain
and sun and clouds
which pass through their windows.

Blessèd are those under a sky covering
as leaves cover trees
in full flower
the life and death of men,
they were like fruit
how good its look how sweet its taste.

Thirty years maybe sixty
the life and death of men
blessèd are those scattered with the sky
mounted on clouds
through their windows pass
thirty maybe sixty years
and the leaves heap up over them leaf
by leaf like stone on stone and the wind calls them by name
and no one knows they're gone.

"Ḥayyim u-frida anashim," Narqisim, p. 32

To His Dust

Just a moment. A moment.
He's been gathered to his dust,
to their dust he's been gathered.
Man, be at peace.

A moon lemon-soft celebrates
or good morning.
A sun turns golden or
good night.
Good night

The rest will do you good,
sometimes oblivion pauses, rest.
My dread has vanished in your dust.
Man, be at peace.
In their dust.

"La-afaro," *Narqisim*, p. 34

Closeness: A Biographical Résumé

From *Yeḥasim udea'ga* (Relations and Worry, 1986)

1

My maternal grandparents were sent to the ovens.
My father was a baker by trade—
on this side and on that bread and ash.

Like a bud cut from a branch I look at the fabric of sky
like a scrap of something whole.

2

A picture without features:
on the right side or on the left inhaling
the colorless wind
standing in that desolate space—
my maternal grandparents, brothers and sisters,
whom I never knew,
unrecorded in the unfamiliar landscape
which leaves no trace.
That space I fill with my own imaginative trajectory,
which reveals something about me
but little, too little, about them.
To their left or to their right
my paternal grandfather was sketched in broken lines,
colored dark. I've no idea where he's from,
but can guess where he's going. My father,
who died before his mother, bequeathed me
the power of forlorness. I keep it whole,
for the moment, like a full-boughed tree, but morning, too,
is spacious, pure as light.
My grandmother did not travel far, I've often seen her
but her speech was strange to me. Even then I've seen
her face lined in old age
and nothing more. My father's sisters and his brother
are more real in their daily toil; what spare
knowledge the world supplies us, even in closeness,

is like saying that even the known is only an assumption,
like taking breath to be the colorless wind
in a picture without features.
the lines of her face in old age
and nothing more. My father's sisters and his brother
are more real in their daily toil; what spare knowledge
the world supplies, even of what's at hand,
like saying the known is only an assumption,
like breathing to be a colorless wind
in a picture without features.
I miss the vivid green,
but surely something must flow from generation to generation
even when the face's secret rests in the shadow of light.

3

In me, it seems, there's a rustic impulse;
it's a fact; an inner order directed
me northwest to Ireland, Scotland,
and I'm still ready for routine adventures
whose externality says little about listening for
the inner conversation
hidden in the living, the growing, gazing forth
from a primeval chain of being.

I was born in a city that broke through to her sun
from virgin sands, and these sands
I never touched for the sake of
archeology. In this city
where sand spreads like a disease in the iron of foundations,
eating away the wall,
this city where hotels collide
in the sea wind and
take the breath away
like an employer from his employee,
in this city my mother put
a shell on the luncheonette counter
so that I'd hear the voice of her relatives lost for all time
whom I'd never know.

The utter silence inscribed in the face of the fisherman, a primitive,
in a place no evil hand had cast a shadow over,
pounded in me. I think of the generations of
ancient beasts steering their life far
between icebergs in the Bering Sea, and of
my lack of the courage to stand in their midst—
fear of the cold pervades me like a thick darkness.
I'll make do with a lake, a hillside, a cloud broken
on the mountaintop like smoke spiraling up from a crater,
and in the inner voice alive in me there is something of belonging
but I don't know, truly I don't, what it means.

"Qirva: tamtsit biografit" *Yehasim udea'ga*, pp. 11–15

News of Home

1

Whether sun or electric light
when the wall of the wall
speaks to the wall of the body
and there is no light.

On the wall I decided where
to hang the picture of oranges,
so in its wanderings it would guide
the seas of light in the shrunken distance.

In time dust has stuck to the frame,
in time a gray stain has spread over
the oranges' wrapping.

Soaked with bitter juice
overnight the oranges lose .
their golden glow, like a waking dream,
like a tremor amidst everyday life.

To turn the gold golden
you must restore the dream
to the bosom of night, far from the daily grind,
distant from the doorway.

2

Time adds little, gives little
and ruins slowly. Here, with the stain stubborn,
cigarette smoke shakes walls,
destroys them. Suddenly, as quickly as the closing of an eye,
the oranges radiate a sublime light.
Thus, like a bird in flight, the body's joy and the spirit's
unite on my threshhold, take wing on my threshold.

And later, open-eyed, it
sinks.

3

In the corner of the porch, between inside and outside,
hidden between the legs of a table stands
a basket filled with love letters.
I was about to reach out when the letters flew off into the air.
I'm dreaming again about the oranges,
locking the door, sinking into the gray stain.

4

On the inside of the closet
I've found a passport photo of my former
wife. I had no money for a photo of the wedding,
neither the first nor the second. Love is not purchased:
Whether it passes or not
no photo can be its witness.

"Hadshot habayit," *Yeḥasim ude'aga,* pp. 50–51, 53–54

Louise's Hour of Song
From *Goral hagan, 1960–1976* (Fate of the Garden, 1989)

Young lady Louise
the mirror sings
the Symphonie Fantastique
of her beautiful years,
little princes of expectation pass through
her sweet sleep, she'd never dream
a thought other than what she'd believed in
when her proud lover, upon leaving, said,
with little sentimental grace,
  "I love you." How mightily young lady Louise
has loved, still
feeling the approach of spring.

Time is no
crueler than a thought about the negligence
of an athletic body thinks sweet Louise
going down to the shore to bathe. She's aware
one must be rigorous at playing music. She knows
the current fashion and clips magazine tours
to go down to small ports of great loves, maybe
to set aside a small fund for autumn days,
so say the champions of memory
and the good life.

This is little Louise's
hour.
This is little Louise's hour of song.
What long distances Louise's grandmother
now travels in magazine photos.
The daily paper's tumult is remote from old age,
the serene tumult of beauty, says Louise,
looking at her mother who's no longer
as she was, in those beautiful days,
when no lines ruled her face,
caught in a passerby's glance.

But the ousted autumn will yet conspire,
who will tell young lady Louise
that the ousted autumn will not lie in ambush.
Maybe then the smile that is love's meaning
will be understood. But who,
who will be bold enough to tell Louise
of conspiracy.

"She'at hashir shel Louise" Goral hagan, pp. 34–35

At the Hour of Illumination

At six o'clock in spring
Louise a dream girl hand
in hand with her lover avenues she'll cross
and she'll resemble, and she'll fully resemble
the sun.
And in the corner of the city's main street
at a small kiosk she'll drink and resemble a glass of sun. But
if she goes a few houses away I'll show Louise dream girl
the land of shadow,
I'll show her the land of shadow,
I'll show Louise dream girl the land of shadow
at the hour of illumination.

"Bishe'at hahitbaharut," *Goral hagan*, p. 42

To My Love, When She Awakens

Quietly quietly the evening passes
in the tree and in the heart. The earth,
a face she renounces heaven's blessing and a cold blast
of wind will disperse
the magic graying in the fallen leaves and announce
good news to seeds hoping for water
to reach the thirsty roots. Quietly

Quietly in my love. Come once more
come once more to your magic my love, come once more
your angelic face veiled, your angelic face is my love,
it rests on isles angels and light
we'll open flowers they'll go, in their grace sailing
away on the seas,
and the heart alone invents their envy of the angels at rest
on isles, in the isles evening

passes quietly quietly. The earth,
a face she renounces and the blast of wind will freeze in the clear air
for my love when she awakens.

"Le'ahavati, keshetashkim." *Goral hagan*, p. 49

On Your Heart, Open

In a city without sky its repose a refuge
I see my years as a shroud
and all the rivers run on all
the rivers run on into the heart all
the rivers and mountains roundabout and all
the rivers rise from their sources
and I how little
of the water I've put in a basket,
a tiny gift, like

water the heart bears on the flower of a kiss
and I a bird on the mountains kissing my mortality
in a city spread out like sky
and the water in pain.

The painful water,
I'll cleave the pain of the painful water,
like a fish slicing through it,
I'll mount the steps of the water
like a bird

on the blue-garbed earth I'll plant a kiss

"Al levavkha, patua<u>h</u>," *Goral hagan*, p. 75

Darkness Turning Sweet

A city have I, I have a sun
a sun have I
on the fruited tongue sweetness trembles with silken skin
and its resonant soul celebrates my coming.

A city have I and the sun's slits have ripened in purity,
a sun have I
a many-toned song have I dreamt for it
and on its heart rests sorrow and all of it is heart.

A city of I its dwellers are mine,
its roofs and balconies stroll in a gentle breeze,
as for me I've sung a city as a legacy.

The earth was perfect for burial, the sea was perfect too,
the wind was beautiful.
a sorrow festive with the seal of darkness turning sweet.

"Hasheikha timtaq," *Goral hagan*, p. 92

In Thicket Sweetness

A waxen land
its evenings chill, its waters
night. He who comes and goes in thicket sweetness shall say
under thatching the sun is a wish,
may your evenings be more blessed than the sun, o mercy.
He who leads me beside the still waters as a legacy
may he make sweet the fruit and give thicket light
and be it said it is good.

"Bemeteq sevakh," *Goral hagan*, p. 108

Toward Night

Overhead a heaven
in which I sit tying clouds and crowns together,
rainbow winds surge through
the watery habitations, blowing fruit
with festive joy.

I've seen mortals
call out to the wind come, come o wind
blow into us the breath of life
and the wind comes toward them
touching but they touch not.

Has the light gone out or

while sleep wraps me round does the mystic speech
pour light forth for calamity.
Look I've seen a dove in flight
open like splendor,
I've seen a dove, but look, it's stone.
I've heard a dove weep in secret
its wing a pool of light.

And black as the eye of darkness
gladdens those who walk toward night.

"Ad layla," *Goral hagan*, p. 119

Songs for Ada

1

Ada assembles songs
and she's the sea never full
she's the sea silencing sorrow.

Ada assembles songs
and every soul will praise the sea.

2

In my sweet sleep he's awake,
a crown whirls around the bird and the blossom,
hurting my eyes.
The children of the hillock and the street, the rustle and the riot,
and above all love, in the sweet sleep
they silence tears.
A man arises like a song: happy art thou,
loveliest of women, a song.

3

Wind moves on the wings the margins of light.
The lilies are all dark. All the lilies.
That light seemed like night,
its companions the winds gazed upon it,
loved it, reviled it,
summer, fall, winter,
its springs are a broken heart
and the lilies at sunrise flower once more.

4

Bread, water and grief.
a colloquy of lilies its hands a look.
A mighty man a hero
he has eyes like a many-colored canopy.
I was telling a tale of the night sky
and the sky was turning dark in that tale.

As if I'd told a tale of the soul going forth
the clouds were turning black
and haughty,
their height and pride ascended.
The tale begins expecting
the waters of love.
The stars were deployed overhead
as over the gateway to hell.

5

A great bird stationed in the sky, a great bird overhead.
A great roar in its wings.
A wondrous experience was lost to me, with its hidden tears
covering with strong sunlight the cup of my heart:
the light be your bedchamber and your dark repose or
your sepulchre and eternal light be yours
and should your daylight be your night the light rise upon you.
Interpret my silence, look,
stationed in the sky is a great bird, a great bird overhead
and from its wings death with a swish will send a wind into the heart's
    drapes and the wind it will return in you.
Look, death touching death.

6

Ada assembles songs
and every soul will praise the sea.

Goral hagan, pp. 145–47

Uncollected

From "Yair Hurvitz: Last Poems"

Just when the body grew cool, and the sun
was at its apex, a soft orange moon
came to me in a dream.
The grief fell away because it was cool,
then I was glad
that a flame burst into my dream,
then I was glad
that the lost was found.
It was then I heard a faint tune
like solace to my soul.

Maybe at midday I'd known
a dream like a cloudburst.
Slowly, the rivulets ran as if gathered
into still pools,
quiet,
unseen in the flood.

Just when the body grew cool, a full moon descended, breathing hard,
back to the source of the malady
that would not take its leave.
It came back, like a persistent threat,
orange, dreamlike, over me and in me.

"Shirim aharonim," *Siman Qri'a*, Vol. 20 (1990), p. 11

Admiel Kosman

ADMIEL KOSMAN was born into a religious "Mizrahi" family at Haifa in 1957. A 1988 graduate of Bar Ilan University with highest honors, he has a Ph.D. degree in Rabbinic Studies and since 1991 has held the rank of Lecturer in the Faculty of Talmud. His research focuses on sociological and historical issues in the period of the Talmud.

The family moved several times, to Ofakim in the Negev, to Ashkelon, Kfar Saba, and Jerusalem. His father worked in the textile business. Kosman attended Orthodox schools and served in the Artillery Corps. After his discharge he studied at the Bezalel School of Arts in a program of graphics and pottery. Later he studied at several Orthodox yeshivot and also studied with the eminent Talmudist, Rabbi Adin Steinsaltz. All in all he had fifteen years of study in Talmud and other texts.

Kosman is a conservative religionist who combines religion and the arts. He is interested in Buddhist meditation and the philosophy of Buddhism. He is married to a woman who converted to Judaism and is involved with music. They have three sons and one daughter who has Down's Syndrome.

He began reading modern poetry at sixteen. The late Amir Gilboa, a prominent poet, published Kosman's first book.

For several years Kosman has been writing a column in the literary pages of the *Ha'aretz* newspaper, with notes on sociological and historical perspectives regarding the world of Judaism.

To date Kosman has published seven collections of his poems. He was awarded the Bernstein Prize in 1990 and the Prime Minister's Prize in 1992. He is the editor of the anthology *Shira hadasha* (New Poetry) with Meron Isackson and several poems of his have been translated into English and French.

Kosman has stated that he had written "true poems" early in his childhood and quickly matured into published writings. To him poetry is "a loving mother, who slowly teaches you to love the travail of poetry." Kosman perceives in poetry "a deep, lucid understanding, accompanied by a personal contentment."

In his work as a university teacher, and in his home, family, and society, he maintains a religiously conservative life. In recent years, however, this has not inhibited him from looking into other religious cultures, especially Buddhism, seeking ways of equipoise and serenity. Yet Kosman craves more than a placid existence. He is in search of a more liberal outlook via his poetry.

He possesses a deep sensibility, a gift for sensual expression, a sharp aesthetic eye, a firm control of his art. Many of his poems exhibit a pictorial character : "an arrow at the heart of the falling sun into the sea," "a cruel clock," "screams are growing . . . on the stone walls of my room" at the burial of a young soldier. In "A Delicate Net Lace of Death," he meditates on his grandmother and her delicate "porcelain life."

Kosman's poetry often mirrors everyday scenes: a picture of a soldier on a postcard, a fatal accident on the highway, a young girl riding in the car with a new piece of jewelry, a flashback to studying contentedly in a room in Jerusalem, a photograph of a love scene with a tree in the background.

Many of the poems portray family images and reflections: Kosman's grandfather and his eucalyptus; the aroma of his grandmother's chicken soup; her illness and death after survival in Europe and migration to Israel; his mother in the kitchen; his wife's thirty-second birthday; the poet playing the piano; having a picnic in a meadow in springtime; a letter from his father; a son's first birthday; a son maturing; the "still life of his wife" on a summer morning.

Kosman's is a voice unlike any other in Israeli poetry fifty years after the establishment of the State.

And After the Fright of the Poem's Making

From *Ve'aḥarei mor'ot mas'aseh hashir*
(And After the Fright of the Poem's Making, 1980)

And after the fright of the poem's making
after the wild scandal of its birth, what's left
these are the graphic signs on the earth
of the chalk scars that police who surrounded
the site of my blasted corpse, a warm bullet
still quivering in the ground, and some people
are whispering about what happened here,
after the terrifying din, after the gathering dispersed.

Ve'aḥarei mor'ot ma'aseh hashir, p. 11

Go Forth

From *Bigdei hanasikh* (The Prince's Clothes, 1988)

For my son Abraham, one year old

Go forth
from here to the light without grabbing hold of the lintels of the
    house and
looking back at the moon-like pallor of your father's face
he's playing music
alone, inside, in the darkness of
the drapes.

To the light, my son, go forth.
You'll be strong. You'll be humble.
The wicked kingdom will be dried up during your life
and peeled away like plaster.

"Tse," *Bigdei hanasikh*, p. 9

Soldier

An arrow at the heart of the sun falling into the sea over Kfar Saba.
Its discharge a greasy trail. Dark red.
And mother's in the narrow kitchen.
A small drawing.
You sketch on a small postcard, sending it
to Goshen,[29] before you, from you to you, go, you
say to it, go away, dove.

From the window as in a frame: military khaki shirt and
pants dripping upside down to the ground, like a cruel
clock, the sum of dissolving minutes for you, a young
soldier of longing, in the palm of the hand.

Summer 1979

"Hayal," *Bigdei nasikh*, p. 23

Just a Short While Ago They Buried Him

Just a short while ago they buried him
and now the screams are climbing
up the stone walls of my Jerusalem room.

Below they've already turned off the light and
the wind still roars
and wails his name
among the pines of Givat Shaul.[30] Cruelly,
it gags on the frightful story about this boy
about the blood and the screams and the body laid out.

"Lifnei sha'a qavru oto," *Bigdei nasikh*, p. 25

A Delicate Lace Net of Death

A delicate lace net of death spread over my sick grandmother's bed.
Delicate and decorated, antique. Stretched muslin, she explains,
in crowded cuneiform writing, notched knife writing,
intricate, in her full handwriting until this
very day, strange things hard to decipher, the events of her life.

Now the hard earth of her new land splits open and slowly gathers
her into it. My grandmother who again is migrating to another new
　　land. Now my grandmother, my grandmother,

the unbroken stone obelisk, says nothing.

When our relatives surround her with good things with bowed heads
　　of bonbonnières, with rustling tops of silver foil, and they have
　　good words.
And kisses on her mouth to revive her.
And I peek below, under the bedposts, and see

The tips of the bristly ankles of the Angel of Death.

"Reshet ta<u>h</u>ra adina shel mavet," *Bigdei nasikh*," p. 26

I Don't Sway When I Pray

I don't sway when I pray. I stand there cold and stiff. Intent on
what's next. Thoughts climb on me silently, like an army of terrorists,
they're quickly caught on the tips of stones, striving onward.

I don't sway when I pray. I stand there cold and stiff. It's been implanted
in me long since the destruction, the desolation, and if I've said I
don't sway
when I pray, and yet inside the hard earth is like rock to me, split,
broken, howling like an oncoming storm bringing calamity.

I don't sway when I pray. I throw my keychain into the air[31] and put
on a dead man's face. Cold and stiff.

"Eineni mitno'ai'a bish'at hatefila," Bigdei nasikh, p. 57

Many Years Later

To my teacher, Rabbi Shimon Gershon Rosenberg, "Shagar"

Many years later in the Jerusalem room
you find yourself clear and finer air.
And good thoughts fall to you
like ripe fruit, contentedly,
into a bed of peaceful leaves.

You look out the window tasting
and again tasting the words
like sweet honey.

Lines of circular silence, a delicate porcelain life
which was not hurt, to be broken, of the vessels
cast aside, to the mottled
shadow wall, blinding the outside of a stone-
land, devoured by its populace.

"Aharei shanim rabot," *Bigdei nasikh*, p. 70

Tall and Long Falls Your Shadow

Tall and long falls your thin Jewish shadow in the
alleys of the Old City face
veiled sparse pointy beard on the windows walls
doorways in the silent pensive night
on the doorlock of a foreign temple
in the pale turquoise light
in the narrow passageway suddenly
in so strange a way your thin
Jewish shadow is broken
and deflected to the wall.

Jerusalem 5747 (1987)

"Gavo'ah mo'orakh nofel tsilkha," *Bigdei nasikh*, p. 79

What I Can
From *Ma ani yakhol* (What I Can, 1995)

I can write poems out of sand, water, and mud.
I've also written poems on the table out of
        small pieces and crumbs of words.
I can write pounding poems.
Strong. Like the shutters. Forceful.
Poems out of rain. Also poems out of tin for the poor.
I can write you fantastic poems out of pieces
        of cotton and send them to you.

I can write you nice poems from the porch.
Giant poems like bundles of hay, higher than clouds.
I can write you wonderful landscape poems while
bending over a platter
or brushing out a filthy sink in a hole of a galley.

My screaming wife and children
are standing down below like a circus of happy faces and I
rise to the water like a word acrobat. Crystals
boil here in my mouth.
Mixed into a thick soup of words.
Right now I'm writing poems out of pieces of potato

Sickly poems
destructive damaging tearing poems about my childhood
about shame and exceptional
sensitivity but I can write you at one stroke like then as if
                        it was nothing

A series of decorative poems. I'm getting up and
                        waving them

like multi-colored ribbons for the echoing
                        laughter of children

Easy poems. Simple poems.
I'm wishing I could write you poems to order
national poems,
march poems, power poems
nice poems about my wonderful gardens
cleverly opening tonight for parties
the soft body pleasure and passion
holy poems dirty poems phooey!
Prayer poems and entreaty poems on all fours
like an animal poems you're-in-a-hurry poems
see, I'm finishing I can
write you even shorter poems than this précis
and in a hurry about a few clinking sugar cubes
and a cup of coffee.

Ma ani yakhol, p. 5

My Love Scene Was Photographed
Facing the Tree

My love scene was photographed facing the tree
a trunk and a treetop shook from excitement.
A bench slowly traveled took off.
And also a bluish sky moved somewhere.

My cruel love scene was photographed
facing the tree. The tree cried from excitement. A bench
took off and crashed, lightning struck, and the sky
turned dark.

My shocking love scene was photographed
facing the tree. The tree bare momentarily naked in the strong
lightning. Me too. A bench stuck confused legs
in the ground, the sky also was startled by it, moved
into the distance, absorbed far off in the warm bosom above.

"Stseinat ha'ahavah sheli tsulma mul ha'ets," *Ma ani yakhol*, p. 9

Girl in the Car

She whispers,
slowly about this
pleasure. Something secretive in the ear. Something
uncoded, uncomprehended, only be

cause she whispers about the pleasure
to her sister in the back seat, something
secretive into the open ear. About a cloak and a
coat, soft golden hair, a *cumaz*.[32]
And with her words she waves the sheet at my feet,
and she discovers,
surely, definitely, that

there's something behind this. She whispers to her, to her sister, in the
    back
seat, by the cloth, her eyes at a distance of only one window,
a window transparent and fastened like muslin
attached by small pins to the soul. A passerby, moves .
the curtain, very gently, like a hint that

there's a fabric, antique, of cloth like this, similar, from India or
China, so fine, not common and cheap like those which cover these
in the streets. A fine white fabric, a Sabbath fabric, a rare fabric, that
    suddenly
will lift life into the air, and fly it to the height of wonder.

Yalda bamekhonit," *Ma ani yakhol*, p. 10

Night Letters to My Sleeping Wife

1. Don't rush. Like a heartfelt commandment:
Don't rush to sleep. Go slow.
Tie up the parched horse of
the body on the mountain slope
to the foot of the wooden table. And close to your sleep
go down to bathe in the lake of the night.

2. Exhaust the night.
The sour dullness of
night. Chew slowly, like tasty green leaves, the essence of night.

3. Hearing a galloping car below before
the night.
This—it saws with a cruel sharpness at the silence of night.

4. The heart of night is halved, flowing bleeding, the criminal of the
    night appears. Horrid.
Across the way in the lower city, his face sealed the victim's face in the
    dark, blazing.
Two equal segments.
Come and see: identical pieces. My face, too, was halved.
And, in the light of the moon it was full of pits. Scars. Knives. Life,
    mocking, called
me. A watermelon of yearnings of the night.

5. O wife, wife of mine, I ride alone on the open summer
window ledge, and a white night moon
sails like a swan, pale, like a knife thrust into the world's flesh, outside,
alone, in the night gloom. Half its heart wholly awake, moist, dripping
sad memories like cold bitter droplets
on the barren
lot
of night

6. But at this time, too, I swallow
up on the motorcycle of the heart
rushed movements of approach
striving toward the depth of night.
Toward the glorious, embracing,
merciful bosom of so much night.

7. Wife of mine, I went forth , envoy, scout delegate,
to discover your darkness, and in the wall
my wife, hidden, buried
in the tunnel of night. I swallow eye
distances from the window of my house,
on the highway stretching into the night. And like a thief, I've
been hidden to my wife, disgracefully, in handcuffs, chained
to the hammer beat of the night, I've already risen
wife of mine, I've climbed up, you come down below

8. See, I've quickly swallowed up
distances soaring in flight.
So close to you
as I come down from the window of night.

9. You are the great iron wing, my wife, and you are the delicate butter-
     fly flitting
about me, and you are the night lamp. You are the carpet that carries
     the body and
you are the city of lights sparkling below at night. You are the moun-
     tain peaks, you
are the cliffs and you are the sea and you are the sand and you are the
     silken wind
joining me with the caress of the flight of night.

10. Distances I have gone! Incredible distances, my wife. Suddenly you
     were a
daughter of distances, and our children were sons of distances, and I
     was a father
kneeling by the roadside and giving birth to the myriad of distances.

11. The distances and distances of distances
distances distances incredible distances
strewn over the vast canvas of the night.

12. That's it, I wasn't afraid, I outstripped myself,
throwing my hat into the air, I cried out: hurray hurray,
slipping from under you and shouting among the myriad night stars.

"12 Mikhtevei layla el ishti hayesheina," *Ma ani yakhol,* pp. 12–15

Apology

From *Semartutim rakim* (Soft Rags, 1990)

A bouquet for a thirty-two-year-old woman

I have sinned, caused sorrow, and tormented, for naught, I confess, your
　　sensitive nervous system, chains, and you've not been able to find a
　　cure from all the words. I see. From here I see
well your soft and melting look. I'm
exchanging it for this fluid, foul look of mine.
Rising from amid the blades of grass, facing you,
I'm continually uplifted like a green
pure everlasting savage, wife of mine,
the hilt of my years is caught in the palm of your years,
like fresh wood, a staff, full and attached, and therefore I am
a spike, heavy-iron, hooks, a swinging axe
and therefore also a bit more cruel,
my behavior uncivilized.

"Hitnatslut," *Semartutim rakim*, p. 10

We Reached God

From *Higa'nu leilohim* (We Reached God, 1998)

We reached God.
Quite by accident. Actually, we stumbled on him.
We were halfway along, on the mountain slope,
with a whole laden donkey train,
and suddenly at a bend in the road,
when we turned aside to look,
we stumbled on him.
He, it happened, had been looking for us,
like a precious stone, he said, like a pearl,
really, like something lost, when quite by accident,
utterly by accident, we were halfway along and reached
the promised land.
Namely, we reached God.
And we found full respite from life.
This was quite by accident, I mean we were halfway along,
when we came down the mountain,
the donkeys with their saddle bags stood alone
untethered and kneeling, at a narrow bend.
The heat was intolerable.

At the end of the path we stumbled on him. Walking back and forth.
He was actually standing in the middle of the road.
Walking back and forth.
Not at a fast pace, but light as a feather, in the corner,
at the edge of the path, we stumbled on him, in his desperate quest
for the precious stone. For the pearl.
We, for our part, were already halfway along, and turned aside to go
    back.

Maybe we'd seen a pit. Maybe we'd seen a waterhole
and momentarily turned from the path.
But the heat was intolerable and the world was on fire like an oven.
And then, as if all heaven opened before us at the tug of a zipper.

And fed our burning eyes
with what no human being, no mortal had seen since
God created Adam to rule
over this arid earth.

Higa'nu leilohim, pp. 5–6

A Tiny Pillar of Fire

The house is filled with chariots of fire.
New horses of fire have arrived.
On the rug lies a giant bar of fire.
And overhead soft white clouds have
blown, fleece-like, a tiny pillar, a torch of fire.

Only then did the treetop rise over us like a date palm.
A giant wave, a clean giant cloud, pure white as a sheet, of fire.
Afterwards, wife of mine, we sat down to a feast of fire.
On the plate, like the First Man and his wife,
together, with deep emotion, we lit
a tiny, dainty pillar of fire.

"Amud qatan shel esh," Higa'nu leilohim, p. 9

We Heard Two Sugar Spoons

We heard two sugar spoons conversing in the void. We joined in.
Again we heard from the edge of the cup, as from exile,
the weeping, the prayers, of grains of sweetness. Scattered, calling out,
    in great emotion, many verses into the emptiness. And again

We joined in. This time the movement was sharp and cruel as a knife.
We went down with the spoon right into the water and punched away.
               At its head. Like
fish. But in vain. The sound was thick. Lost. Dry like this.
Battered. And still God's faint voice was rising from below. Seeking.
As if groaning or whispering.

          "Sham'anu shtei kapiyot sukar," *Higa'nu leilohim*, p. 12

One Moment

They're mentioning me now, wife of mine,
in one breath, together with the day
and with the night. I'm mentioned together
with the sun. The moon. The host of stars.
They're mentioning me now in one breath
with the soft air girdling the universe.

"Rega e<u>h</u>ad," *Higa'nu leilohim*, p. 13

Piyyut[33]

(To be recited on the Days of Awe
based upon a terrible event
that befell the writer and his wife,
may she live long,
on the Ninth of Tammuz 5745)[34]

I'll send it by FAX and I'll be brief
not to disturb you blessèd Creator of time
Creator of the past of the future Creator
of everything Creator of the varieties of fruits
Creator of the fruit of the earth blessèd Creator
of sorrows Creator of all beauty in its seasons

Blessèd Creator, awesome, mighty in deeds
Creator of the kinds of shrieks and screams
Creator inventor genius renewer
of the slender, delicate kinds of disgrace
on high here below in the whole universe
Creator of wood Creator of iron Creator of paper
Blessèd Creator, you've glued it all together

Creator of the fruit of speech love
coupling Creator of the blind
Creator of the deaf Creator of lovely
varieties, great, healthy, new, of violence in the marketplace
Creator of the kinds of sex of sexual intercourse
of lovemaking Creator of the kinds of positions
Creator of the kinds of moans wafting within
with powerful artistry like the winds, everything beautiful in its seasons

Blessèd Creator, awesome, mighty in deeds
Creator of the kinds of shrieks and screams
Creator inventor genius renewer
of the slender, delicate kinds of disgrace
on high here below in the whole universe

Creator of wood Creator of iron Creator of paper
Blessèd Creator, you've glued it all together

Creator of devils and angels and servants all their assigned times
their varieties for day for night and for ample ways of space on the mirror
on the bed on the chest on the bureau blessèd blessèd are you blessèd
Creator of the fruit of silence blessèd Creator of the varieties of fear
    terror quaking
the varieties of malice
and the vice of those who dress in style a trim dress
like muslin, sheer, cunning, of pure design
oval curved, a lovely cut,
for the nakedness of the living virgin blessèd blessèd blessèd are you
blessèd Creator of mud within blessèd
Creator of mire

Blessèd Creator, awesome, mighty in deeds
Creator of the kinds of shrieks and screams
Creator inventor genius renewer
of the slender, delicate kinds of disgrace
on high here below in the whole universe
Creator of wood Creator of iron Creator of paper
Blessèd Creator, you've glued it all together

"Piyyut," *Higa'nu leilohim*, pp. 26–27

I Roll Out the Hours of the Day
and the Hours of the Night

I roll out the hours of the day and the hours of the night.
Here, I'm momentarily a little god. You won't believe it, even
when I'm all-powerful I treat all humankind
with great solicitude, and provide for them abundantly.
The hours of leisure I set aside for activity:
wisdom, understanding and charity, glory, majesty, and so on.

Here, I've become a little god.
If you look out the window overhead,
you'll see me sitting on the throne.
You won't believe me when I roll like dice—
I'm the roller—your future, the hours of the day and the hours of the
    night.
Though sometimes I stop.

I stop a moment and say all at once: "Let there be light!" And light
    there is!
Or at day's end I say the opposite: "Let it be dark,"
and suddenly—over the waters hovers this terrifying shadow.

But it's with great solicitude, gentleness, sensitivity
and regard for their acute vulnerability I treat humankind, dwellers
in the clay houses, down there, below me—
and, for the most part, provide for them abundantly.
So I nourish my world, each creature according to its needs,
from the legendary ox to the tiny eggs of lice.

I seize the hours of the day
rolling them out by hand like dice
and with a blow open for each nation the gates of its fate.

"Ani megalgel she'ot hayom ushe'ot halayla," *Higa'nu leilohim*, pp. 32–33

Poem

Look, silence is melting between the evening's breasts
rising over it in huge soft clouds, over the sheet
of the horizon. A bit under it, down below, as if bisecting
the world, with a burning red line, the strong stripe
of the day's underwear stripped off.

On the sky, already written in ink, forbidden secrets.
Ten commandments inscribed, given the people as a gift.
Explained. Explained and severe without parallel. No none
can any longer wander in the realm of risk!

But below, listen, really below and out of bounds, right under
God's nose is a poet. Trembling. Thin. Pale.
Crawling—like an tiny lizard—under the fence,

Into the heart of darkness changing color. Climbing slowly—
because he's blind—over the wall. Writing in huge shocking graffiti,
word by word, the whole poem. Right under God's nose—Do you
    hear? Right under his nose—
come these cursèd lines!

"Shir," *Higa'nu leilohim*, p. 43

Song of Devotion

Strike again and again, thus and thus and thus, in faith and devotion.
To fulfill to the letter the commandment of the Lord of lords:
the great mighty and awesome God—who does not discriminate; the
    God who delivers nations, peoples; the God who stirs small shoots,
    of continents, islands; the God who wars with our rivals—among
    the dead and living. He is our island God
—Elohenu—lordy Lord.

While gleaning seeds
tossed up on the seashore we remembered
the childhood drops of blood; the silence of parents;
teachers, leaders;

We remembered in devotion.
And suddenly we remembered even the gentle
God, sheltering the innocence
of youth, assuredly,
the savior—our lordy
Lord.

And at once—unwaveringly—
we arose! For zealous are we
to fulfill a commandment! And we took with us
huge knapsacks,
and enveloped in hatred we beat up
wayfarers happening by.

Strike again and again, thus and thus and thus, in faith and devotion.
To fulfill to the letter the commandment of the Lord of lords:
the great mighty and awesome God—who does not discriminate; the
    God who delivers nations, peoples; the God who stirs small shoots,
    of continents, islands; the God who wars with our rivals—among
    the dead and living. He is our island God
—Elohenu—lordy Lord.

While gleaning seeds tossed up
on the shore—suddenly we remembered sex. Yes,
the particulars-of-the-commandment-of-sex, sweet gentle sex—
the relaxed sex of parents; while quite accidentally gleaning
seeds the sea had tossed up on the shore, we remembered our beloved
parents, who brought us here. With sex. The rich heritage
of our parents—cruel intruders who bequeathed us a True-Faith in all
    the
mighty force of dream;

The first and the first of the first and the giants of giants who overran
    the shore initially as angels, in the guise of Adam and Eve; and
    thereby bequeathed us,
children of the island, the might of passion-blood;

And we took up a round club. A holy club.
A huge round club—brought to the island
in the age of ancestral conquest, a club of faith, fidelity, root; years ago,
so many years ago, a mighty club of gentleness; when the first and the
    first of the first who overran the ancestral shore, Chaldeans from
    Ur—took with them in urns fragments of a club; a huge club. A
    huge round club, brought
with them here to the passion shore in a storm of conquest and love,
    years ago;

A huge club;
a club of memories,
a club of gentleness and yearning; a club brought with them in
crowded-tearful-wandering from exile; a holy club; an oaken club,
a huge club topped by a knob. A knob
crowned with iron; a crossbeam pinned to a dagger.

Thus, we struck and wounded all wicked peoples, children of abomina-
    tion; wayfarers happening by who'd been suddenly tossed up like
    seaweed-dropped
gently, gliding on the waves; in the bosom of
this semi-pastoral island, beneath the palms.

Strike again and again, thus and thus and thus, in faith and devotion.
To fulfill to the letter the commandment of the Lord of lords:
the great mighty and awesome God—who does not discriminate; the
God who delivers nations, peoples; the God who stirs small shoots,
of continents, islands; the God who wars with our rivals—among
the dead and living. He is our island God
—Elohenu—lordy
Lord.

" Shir hadevequt," *Higa'nu leilohim,* pp. 51–53

Letter to a Far Off Village, Over the Snow-Capped Peaks of Sex

From *Perush Hadash, b'sad* (A New Commentary with
God's Help, 2000)

We'll be sending you men and women instructors, on request.
OK?
Instructors good for the body.
Excellent instructors.
Who'll teach you all to fly.
And our instructors will teach you
positions.

To fly: namely, to fly into a wondrous
cloud. A cloud: namely, a wonder of wonders. To fly:
high, in the mountains, with a crew of men and women instructors. A
    long
flight, an astounding flight, over the snow-capped peaks of sex.

Positions: namely, a range
of positions. Coital positions. They'll teach
you how to caress each other and embrace and love, a warm
touch, how to dress each other, how to undress each other,
how to sigh, how to moan. How
to vanish in a flash like a huge
bird into the haze of tenements.
Into a fine white screen,
soft and delicate, of clouds.

They'll teach you all sorts of things.
They're willing to stay in this village
a great many years.
You'll all sit and write down
everything in little notebooks,
in meticulous script
filled with little drawings:

To fly: namely, to fly into a wondrous
cloud. A cloud: namely, a wonder of wonders. To fly:
high, in the mountains, with a crew of men and women instructors. A
    long
flight, an astounding flight, over the snow-capped peaks of sex.

But, as in solitude, a long hard journey will be required of you.
To childhood. In a dense script. Like
cuneiform, full of episodes. With the body's pencil
we'll write God a sad, anguished letter.

In a small script, quite small,
of the lost, like the echo of a scream,
in the downfalls of grownups. Everything
so beautiful, on a memorial tablet.
You'll sit like children.
On chairs. With backs bent over.
And from the body instructor's
mouth you'll write down a whole
lot of little shapes and signs.

To fly: namely, to fly into a wondrous
cloud. A cloud: namely, a wonder of wonders. To fly:
high, in the mountains, with a crew of men and women instructors. A
    long
flight, an astounding flight, over the snow-capped peaks of sex.

"Mikhtav likhfar rahoq, me'al harei hasheleg shel hamin,"
Perush Hadash, pp. 34–35

Yitzhak Laor

YITZHAK LAOR, born at Pardes Hannah in 1948, currently lives in Tel Aviv. He earned his B.A. and M.A. degrees in theater and literature from Tel Aviv University, and has completed his doctoral dissertation in the University's Department of Hebrew Literature.

Laor's parents emigrated to the Palestine Mandate separately in 1934. His father, a native of Bielfeld, Germany, had been a member of a Socialist youth movement. His mother, who came from Riga, Latvia, was a member of Beitar, a rightist nationalistic Zionist youth movement. During World War II, Laor's father served in the British Army for six years in North Africa and Europe.

Laor grew up in Pardes Hannah and did his compulsory service in the Nahal, a program combining agricultural and military duties. A conscientious objector, he was jailed for refusing to serve in the Occupied Territories. His left-wing opinions, expressed in his works, continually nettled the mainstream establishment. In some quarters during the eighties Laor was called the "Bad Boy" of Hebrew literature.

A poem he wrote against the West Bank Jewish settlers aroused many nasty responses. His play, *Ephra'im hozer latzava* (Ephra'im goes back to the army), parodied the anti-heroic novella *Ephraim hozer la'esspesset* (Ephra'im goes back to the alfalfa) that eminent author S. Yizhar had published in 1949. Laor's play was banned by government censorship in 1985, but in 1987 won High Court of Justice approval for performance. Obviously Laor is a provocative antiestablishment person.

He is also an extraordinarily creative, multifaceted artist, involved in several realms of art: poetry, prose, and essayistic and dramatic writing. He has taught in the Department of Theater at Tel Aviv University and later in the Jerusalem School of Film. He regularly publishes literary reviews in the liberal daily *Ha'aretz* and also writes journalistic essays on culture, society, and politics.

Over the last twenty years, Laor has published a variety of books: a collection of short stories, *Outside the Fence* (1981); six volumes of poetry, *Going Away* (1982), *Only the Body Can Remember* (1985), *Poems in the Valley of Iron* (1990), *A Night in a Foreign Hotel* (1992), *And Loveth Many Days* (1996), and *As Nothing* (1999); a play, *Ephraim Returns to the Army* (1987); a collection of essays on Israeli literature, *Narratives with No Natives* (1995); and two novels, *The People, Food Fit for a King* (1993) and *And with My Spirit, My Corpse* (1998).

▨ Many poems by Yitzhak Laor offer images of and references to distance, travel, wandering, crossing borders, exploring various unnamed lands, various cultures, hotels, and foreign cities. The poet projects a sense of restlessness, an impulsive personality, an inability to mingle well with average people. His persona is that of a serious loner, one who constantly wishes to "escape from the ordinary." Despite this limited vision, he would surely say that he has had "a life of abundance."

Laor is adventurous, spirited, even daring. He seems incessantly on the move, his greatest need complete freedom—of thought, work, motion, boldness. In the poem "Distance," the poet asserts, "I could decide whatever I want, only not to stop." Endowed with a volatile emotional temperament, he evinces a forceful obsession with escape from the commonplace. In a "heart-of-darkness" adventure—probably in wartime—he could not say goodbye to a friend, and left him in the darkness of death. He wanted to disappear, to be considered dead himself, to run away; he "surrounded himself with oblivion."

Laor has soft spots in his themes of "yearning" or "pining." Bold as he is, he often "feels he's falling apart." There is also nostalgia, looking back to his mother in childhood and to his father's death. Various other images appear in his poems: the death of a child, a bloody blanket torn by shrapnel, a plane plunging into the sea. There are also more sanguine, sensitive images in these poems: a cloud of butterflies, a plum tree blossoming.

Despite Laor's experience of turmoil, loss, and lament, he craves a "thirst for light," and most of all, he seeks recognition. As he puts it: "a recognizable voice."

Distance

From *Shirim be'emeq habarzel*
(Poems in the Valley of Iron, 1990)

On its belly at the bottom of the dark slithers the train.
Villagers, getting into bed, see its checkered light.
Tonight the river will freeze, the grass will turn white
with frost. A whistle blast pierces the foreign air.
Here you are, asleep in the belly of the great worm.
For a moment you open one eye, see signs of empty
stations, fall asleep again. Borders pass, languages and
conductors' uniforms, and you, an invisible thread
in the fabric. In my room,
I tremble with longing

"Merḥaq," *Shirim be'emeq habarzel*, p. 9

In a Village Whose Name I Don't Know

In a large yard behind the house
at the foot of a very wide tree whose name I also don't know
I've already been sitting half the night. Quiet, grand beauty
surrounds me. Someone's watching and walks away maybe
he didn't quite see me maybe he did but not quite

It's beautiful here. I have no complaints, I'm not
hungry or thirsty, there's time for poetic meditation.
The man who passed close by me in the dark looked
about, saw the overturned barrel lying on its side, he didn't
touch it, he patted a sleepy cat, drank some water from a large pitcher,
turned in the direction of the lighted villages beyond the border, he also
studied them and returned to the door. For a moment I hoped I'd be
    caught
for a moment I thought he might bring in more peasants. But

Inside the house they began to sing, in four parts,
a cappella. I didn't recognize the songs and
don't speak the local language
if he'd asked me to join in I wouldn't
know how to explain my refusal or my marginality
I don't really know how to explain

But all night I sat in the dark under a tree cast in the silvery moonlight
holiness of a summer night, myriads of stars an overturned barrel
peasants singing softly all night long I wanted to be a part
of this beauty not to write about it or

To be a part of it and to write about it but
I was an overturned barrel a cat in the dark a tree a star
A rusty piece of junk within this beauty whose inheritance
has been denied me,[35] nothing will remain with me except for this poem
unless it gets lost or is forgotten

"Bikhfar shegam et shemo eini yode'a," *Shirim be'emeq habarzel*, pp. 12–13

Citizen of the World

We didn't grow up where our ancestors did.
They didn't grow up
where their ancestors did. We've learned not
to yearn (we can yearn for any grave
decided on) we don't belong to any
place (we easily latch onto whatever
is demanded of us) we wander over the face of the
earth, we sleep in fancy hotels, we
sleep in cold barns, we love only to be
loved, we rape only to be remembered, we
enjoy only to claim ownership,
destroy mainly villages, declare ownership and
move on, hate peasants, mainly peasants
(if necessary, we'll even work
the soil)

"Ezra<u>h</u> ha'olam," *Shirim be'emeq habarzel*, p. 46

Foreign Cities

I live among people who don't hate me
don't love me don't even know
I exist. I pass by them, for example
in the street at morning quietly I say to myself
but they don't hear me
like the man clearing his throat next to me. They
quickly go on their way not getting even
one word I've said maybe one syllable
clearing my throat. For a moment I tremble:
"Like a thread of grass in the morning with the wind"
I note poetically to be sure

And I call out my name more loudly
that is I whisper it in this silence
maybe I'm not all awake and if I scream—will they hear?
(and if they respond—will I stay?)
but I'll scream like a dog wailing
why have you forsaken me my voice
will echo my bark will search for an accused to flail
him with defined words organized pain false
wrath an ungrateful accused
as it is with suffering

And I wander the streets of this city like a forced remedy
learning to say I admit only I know how inside me
I live a life of abundance myriads of words like a cage full
of birds swarming in me refusing to know they are non-
existent learning to say I admit that's how it is I see and am un-
seen speak and am unheard loving and unloved even pitying
and unpitied.
And despite it all I have no solace and despite it all
won't forgive the insult and at the end of the streets where my body
　　　and soul

have tired of this tortuous remedy I ask for one reality
to write whence I come and whither I go
and make an accounting only unto myself

"Arim zarot," *Shirim be'emeq habarzel*, pp. 47–48

Mother

We fled from the dashing clouds,
took off our shoes in haste, left them
behind in the desolate outdoors by the
entry with clods of clay soil
my mother was at home and
despite my writing in the first
person plural I don't remember who
fled with me from the heavy rains that came
from the west, from the drowning forest in
the sea-darkness
and who was still there besides us who
came to us for black bread and honey who
came to play alongside the new kerosene stove
by your warmth.

In summer's desolation the smell of rain and the feel of clay soil
and the taste of the water stored by the tangerine leaves
and the sound of the rain beating at the windows, and the look
of the fields in the rain I remember you
and like a blind man I'll forget the sights
and the smells, the memories will fade
like the decades of learning and
the freckles on your hands up to the nipple

"Imma," *Shirim be'emeq habarzel,* p. 59

If There is No God

From *Layla bemalon zar*
(Night in a Strange Hotel, 1992)

If there is a God, He is not in heaven and not the birds
are His myriad eyes, He is One like a bird
like birds. He is the sea gazing at the land like a serpent
speechless. Like the gaping wells of water in the ground
(not one well in the middle of the world). He is the gaze that
identifies human beings and sees the loneliness of hurried breath,
smells the body's rift, hears the semen quickly jostling
into the womb, the blood-tissues swaying so slowly,
He will see, He will call Adam
Adam. If God, then Adam

"Im ein elohim," *Layla bemalon zar*, p. 10

My Babbling, Your Silence, My Father

A small fire still burns in the cold flesh: Bless the living, father
bless the flesh, bless the blood, father, even when the flesh seeps cold
blood, someone human like that, father (and what will you say why did
you bear me, mother? And to whom will you say it?). After decades a
man is more alone than before, when he comes here, surrounded by
those who love him and he gradually loses them, one by one, he alone
remains. Father, father, you're alone in the dark, sole witness to the
turmoil of your life (sons daughters, what do they know? A diet of
sugar or salt, medicine from the health clinic, that they know).
Preserve the testimony, let the memories burn slowly, for they are the
body. Don't summarize, don't judge, don't pry (prying's a sin), let the
memories burn slowly, slowly, no one's sitting with you in the heavy
darkness in which you call out for the memories to come, to be honored,
to be blessed: living, being, fading.

Yarnton Manor, Oxford, November, 1990

"Pitputai, shtiqatkha, avi," *Layla bemalon zar*, p. 11

Listen to Your Voice Coming

For A.K., Love always

The corpse of a vast night covers me, I was formed by the depths
of the land I drowned in a dusty place and like a dog I thirst
for light, for a recognizable voice, for a familiar smell
awake under the blanket, under the dust of darkness I begin to organ-
    ize:
imagining a place to live, imagining a plaza, imagining a story, a protag-
    onist,
a future a past, imagining two or three clear truths
amidst the cave, the rumble, the turmoil, amidst the silence
I'll be seized by the noise of a passing car (and which side is the
sea on?) I'll recognize voices and compare them to others, darkness
to earth and earth to sea and sea to a flow of sea, from there I'd float
in the sun and bleed the dark of the abyss voices and from here
to two or three choruses and all of them in one rhythm beat
(in bed by my body under the same blanket my love's organization
unraveling in the dark)

How sweet the respite, be an accessory (our distant home's safe
insured, the bank account's growing like hay), be a mensch among
menschen, meaning even in the desert quiet hear a voice calling
you, respond Here I am (meaning if I'm not called I don't exist)
organize yourself, hear your voice coming from outside, direct it to the
    other
body, talk to it, talk to yourself (truth is also an artificial island) how I
    yearn
and how I yearn for you
for a place of light

"Shma et qolkha," *Layla bemalon zar*, p. 12

I Won't Strangle You

Someone should track down a certain voice, amid the rumble,
amid the unfamiliar din, amid the silence, perhaps to be caught
in the noise of a passing car, speeding off, in order to be a thing,
a detail, to rest, to move, to wander in a watery sleep
(but look, even the roads around this foreign hotel
I can't sketch for myself). Then you fell asleep, all at once,
as if afloat in darkness somewhere else on the current
(perhaps you'd lain there a bit waiting awake fixing your eyes
on me or the dark) and I peered into space, recognized
nothing, nor could I make out what the tourists are saying
behind the thin wall, if they're arguing or getting excited (the more the stranger
the less you distinguish one word from another). Only I remain
in these depths, and what is not I. You breathe in a rhythm different
    from mine. I thrust away the world from my ears to my eyes and
    beyond. If you'd appease
me I'd be less petrified now, perhaps
asleep like seaweed (O, how many grudges I have
inflaming a baseless hatred instead of consoling you with an apology:
how quietly you've passed into sleep) and you float among bad dreams
like a rudderless ship, amid remnants of a strifeladen evening
in a foreign city. (Where shall we sightsee tomorrow alone or together
silent, unwilling to be parted) I won't strangle you
in your sleep. I know your trusting look which will accept this silently.

Lo eḥnoq otakh," *Layla bemalon zar,* p. 13

Hotel By the Sea

The sea rolls its skin, baring its myriads of pale
bones, grass and shells, soft rock and an iodine stench
rising from the bared earth, the ebbtide ooze
sleeping, we wake with the tide, so slowly
silently rise the waters, maybe crawling is the right word,
a large open eye of a great monster, open, closed, closing,
opening, the sea rises a bloodplague, an awakening
far from the sea, another moving closer
to the sea. We travel the world, restless
unredeemed, we argue, love, abandon
transport a whole household, fold clothes, a few goods
awkward sex, we travel and stop, spread again our
homey smell like a familiar sheet atop a strange mattress. I sleep
wake, go to the window, look at the yellow sea. Maybe I'll escape
from you. If you wake and ask where I'm going, I'll say: Let's
get away from here quickly without taking anything along

"Malon leyad hayam," *Layla bemalon zar*, p. 16

Distance

I drive far for
hours, digging into the dark, distancing myself
on the earth's surface, the earth growing smaller
behind me, it rises in the fire of my headlights, sinks
in the darkness. Boldness overwhelms me, overwhelms
not, passes me by, not boldness, fear
passes me, passes not, drills, seeps, not
fear, a shudder, pierces, pierces not,
crucifies. Where are you flying to, it's just a
trip, not a trip, a pursuit, not a pursuit
an escape, not an escape, devouring, not
devouring, a conglomeration. I look at the
glowing mileage gauge.
How far is the way back. I could crash
myself into the sea, No. I could set
the car on fire. No. Could wallow
in my semen. No. Scream. Quiet in the car
(I drive with deep concentration) I could
decide whatever I want only not to stop

"Ri<u>h</u>uq," *Layla bemalon zar*, p. 25

Songs of the Wanderer

COMPELLED

I lie in the heart of darkness. Maybe I'm a soldier
maybe I'm a hiker, maybe I'm the life
of the soldier/hiker, in any case, I'm
compelled to wander (that is to say, I move on with a strength of sorts
    from one bed
to the next)

MEANWHILE

I didn't mention I left, didn't mention
I arrived, I left in the dark, I came into
the dark, I lie down with a strength of sorts
under the blanket. Day after day, till
the end of days. When the blanket dissolves, I'll be
darkness, meanwhile I move on
fully revealed, intent on disappearing

FORGOT

Whoever knows, knows very little about me, knows only
if he really saw me whole, heard me whole
heard about me whole, from someone who
may have forgotten or died and if he was not dead
maybe he considered I was dead, or
was really someone else. I seem whole, I'm
destined to disappear (surrounded by oblivion)

CONSIDERED

I'll be leaving here in the dark. At the next place
where I'll be lying under the blanket, they'll already
know something else, if they know
something at all (my hair color, the color of
my jacket, happy or sad) actually
I'm considered alive and considered dead

A STORY

Because of this I both move on and talk about
my moving on. Because of this I lie down
and talk about my lying down and I
(alone under the blanket) can tell anyone I want
(whatever I want) every moment the story of my life (even
in the salt dark murky as blood I can tell
the uncompleted story of my life) sometimes I talk
ceaselessly and sometimes I'm silent

KNOWING

So I don't recognize what others
recognize in me (or could have recognized
in me if someone had mentioned me)
but I do recognize my body since then
till now and till the end, my end, my body
wandering about the wide world
from bed to bed
from lair to lair
from lamp to lamp

TRAIN

And as long as I live, lives with me
(not so precise, somewhat distant)
the true story of my life even when I'm silence
forcefully I lie down in the deep salt
darkness (like algae) listening: on a distant track a train
whistles heavy and long

October 1991

Layla bemalon zar, pp. 29–35

Poetry

From *Ohev yamim* (And Loveth Many Days, 1996)

The dead died in summer and the poem
was written in winter and also spring
and fall passed more than once
but I'm writing it again
and again: the dead died in summer
and the poem was written in winter.
I write poetry so
as not to fall apart

And what do I do when I don't write
and how is it that I don't fall apart
despite it all ? Maybe because
poetry is a kind of walking and stopping

(At times I wait for a bus
at the stop, but when it doesn't come, I'm filled
with restlessness and walk up to the next
stop and again I wait and again I
walk on, stop, miss it, come late
slow and in a hurry) I write because I'm
falling apart, I'm a poet at precisely the points
I'm not writing not walking and not even sitting. Where in the great
space is the point with which I am (thinking
of me not writing, falling apart, a poet)

"Shira," Ohev yamim, p. 35

Coral

Slowly the body disintegrates like a large
silhouette of a fish flitting
in the water, look, your life has flitted from you
the flesh amid a gathering of our bodies
these waters and skeletons
like scorching coral or
fruit falling the flesh disappearing

February–March, 1994

"Almog," *Ohev yamim,* p. 36

Fog

It's cold in the house, winter, a house
a dark bubble, the shadowy clothes
I quietly gather
cold as a night watchman.
I'll guard the buzzing, I'll follow it
from room to room, the house is in the fog
the plane is in the fog.
And I'm at home
when the plane crashes
(what sort of house is this
when a plane crashes)

"Arafel," *Ohev yamim*, p. 55

Less and Less

Fewer and fewer people I pine for
despite more and more people disappearing
but the pining is not quenched
it's even more painful.
Less and less the pain,
less do I allow the pining
to mislead, to burst out. That's how I'll die:
writing means pining
writing means living, escaping
from pining (beneath the plane
like white smoke dying out
the heart is filled with rubbery blood
revolving in the body)

"Pahot ufahot," *Ohev yamim*, p. 56

Pining

If I'm going to write, I'll write
my mother, how I called out to her at night
come to my bedside and said what she loved to hear
and she hugged and kissed me
my sweet life, dead mother of mine,
my death, sweetest of all

"Ga'agua," *Ohev yamim*, p. 57

Steel

It's impossible to pine
for someone who won't return. I'm drowsy
like a mouth during a tooth extraction, or
a memory. A piece of shrapnel
cold cutting into the body flooding it
my blood my soft blanket.

And the world's a balloon hovering
in a distant and hot place, sun in the
other half of the world. I don't want
to travel there, and not to anywhere,
and not to see a plum tree blossoming in a place
where now a plum tree stands trembling
like a silent cloud of butterflies.

There are moments
like these, the dark
house is the place
to live in
forever.
I pass through the house,
a bristling cat, not
myself, something
passes through in the house,
in me
a bristling cat
It's not the body that's
weighty, nor is the pain weighty
but what is it that is so weighty
a memory of the blow
a plane plunging into the sea

(but the soul
is not so meager
even if it's
clear)

"Pelada," *Ohev yamim*, pp. 58–59

Window

I'm the one
sitting alone
in the hotel by
a narrow table, smoothing
a hand on a cold page
prepared
to be happy
looking at himself from the lighted
window. That's how happiness
is described with pen
on paper

set down
a heavy
body
asleep, a man
awake, flesh bloodless

"Halon," *Ohev yamim*, p. 66

Room

Next door I'm
unheard hearing
a breath. "You'll be happy,
buy yourself a pen
and paper." I'll be
happy I promised
you, I'll write poetry:
"I'll be happy
among the happy ones
I'll write bunches of
poems." A joyless man
doesn't write poems.
(a poem
is a roach hunt)

Not so: a poem
is cracks in the
wall. I promised
you: I'll be happy
I'll write poems

"Ḥeder," *Ohev yamim*, p. 67

And Loveth Many Days

Milky skies hang like a sheet
outside our window, the smell of milk
drifts in the room from your white skin, your
mother's breast shrivels into your throat, my hair
slips towards your head, my life
is squandered. For hours I sit
looking at you as an infant looks at
a man, eye to eye. What do I know? Yes, being
comes from nothing (the place of breath the soul) but
where shall the being go? Every morning I get up first
thing to come to your room to listen
to the gurgles of your sucking, one by
one, to empty the minutes
of my life into the days of your life (and when you grow up, seek
peace my son, even from your pursuers)

Monday, August 14, 1995

Ohev yamim, p. 117

Bread, Daily

From *Ke'ayin* (As Nothing, 1999)

Our Father which art in Heaven,
Give us this day our daily bread and that's it. Thine
The Kingdom, and the Power, and the Glory
Forever and ours the rich neighbors
Rich friends returning
From abroad with their stories. And lead us not into
Temptation, jealousy and hatred, not because "Thou shalt love thy
      neighbor,"
But because time is short, mind is precious, burning
Is rationed, the ledger is open, the hand is paralyzed
Soon

Forever I shall be the Father
Even when I'm erased from the earth,
I inscribed my fatherhood in my son, who will inscribe
His fatherhood in his son. That's not it. I'm inscribing
In my son my father, who inscribed in me his father, and my son
Will inscribe me in his son. Let my fatherhood be
Only a ghost, not a goad, let my fatherhood be
Motherhood

Above the window the trail of
Milk, kingdom come
Of milk to our mouths, to
The rush of blood in the flesh, in the temples
In the arteries, in the genitalia
In the boy trembling from a milky
Dream.

"Lehem, hoq," p. 17
Translated with the author.

Rivka Miriam

RIVKA MIRIAM is the daughter of Esther and Leib Rokhman, survivors of the Holocaust. Her father, an eminent Yiddish writer (1918–78), was born at Minsk Masovetzky, near Warsaw. He studied in yeshivot and at the age of seventeen was ordained a rabbi. Soon after, he left the life of Orthodoxy and began writing for the Yiddish newspapers in Warsaw. When the Second World War began, he returned to his town, but with the liquidation of the ghetto in 1942, he escaped with his wife and hid in a farmhouse. There Rokhman kept a diary, which was published after the war. At the end of the war he spent several years in Swiss sanitariums, where he was cured of tuberculosis. After a short stay in France, he and his wife emigrated to Israel in 1950. There he worked in radio and continued his writing.

Rivka Miriam went to the Ma'ale religious high school in Jerusalem, since her parents wanted their daughter and son to have the benefit of a full Jewish education. Miriam herself has three children.

Becoming involved in Jewish education, she joined a circle in Jerusalem called Elul, an open adult education association, which focuses on issues of Judaism for both religious and secular individuals. Miriam was also active with the Jerusalem branch of the Association of Hebrew Writers and became the committee chair.

As a poet and an artist, Miriam was recognized for her poetry even in childhood. She began writing poems at the age of seven and, at twelve, began painting. Her first poems were published when she was eight, and her first book was published in 1966, when she was fourteen. She also did the illustrations.

She had a one-woman show of her drawings at the Tel Aviv Museum in 1969 and, in 1979, a show at the grand hall in Ein Harod and in Jerusalem. To date, Miriam has published eight collections of poetry and other writings, including two short story collections and two children's books.

Rivka Miriam's poems present a varied group of forceful and arresting topics and styles. Her works reflect love, sensuality, biblical tales, the mythical Shulamite, King Solomon speaking the language of animals, her own relationship with God, her children, birthings, pleasures, and her father's death.

Much of her oeuvre is idiosyncratic, which in this case engenders great charm, originality, and appeal. For example, "A Circumcised Man and I" pictures an erotic moment; the man "grasps my hips and touches my wings," as if the woman, sensually and mythically, will take flight. The humor and candor much enhance the erotic scene.

A good number of poems present domestic or familial portraits. An especially moving scene is the death of Miriam's father. At the grave on a Jerusalem hill, Miriam invokes her father's death and simultaneously her own birth. Father and daughter are intertwined. She laments, "I have no father!" However, several conception images bring both death and new life together. "I rose in his flowing," Miriam says, "I was sprayed by him," in order to keep her father close.

Images of religion appear in the poet's world. She seems to cherish a personal connection to God. She makes use—sometimes parodistic use— of the traditional liturgy. She calls God "my God," who has given her a soul, which "flows within me like an hourglass," a divinity of time, of many names, of prayers given to her by God. But she proclaims, "I am his God the mighty and awesome"—ironically, she turns and says, "I created him and I can kill him." Who, then, has the power, who worships whom? "A man makes seed," Miriam offers, yet again proclaims, "I am his God, and he is my God." Like King Solomon and his animals and tongues, Miriam has one God, but He goes by different names, shows different faces of the divine.

Poet as protagonist, Miriam inquires about many things. She wants to know when she was born, in the light or the dark? born or died?—child-like queries of unanswerable puzzles. Her personality evinces a full life, strong self-reliance, independence, a love of art, learning, children, dogs, and cats. She also has a need for protection, for privacy (her "empty room" à la Virginia Woolf), especially with her family.

In sum, Rivka Miriam has penned a broad diversity of works, including challenging metaphors, keen ironies, engaging characters, women-and-men issues, a spectrum of scenes from the biblical, mythical, and everyday lives in our contemporary world.

I Unbuttoned My Dress

From *Etz naga be'etz* (Tree Reached to Tree, 1978)

And then
I unbuttoned my dress
and gave birth to my daughter.
Eight dead men erect were rushing me in silence.
And I gave birth to my daughter.
My blood was transparent and massive.
A thin ribbon of linen wound about me.
Eight dead men heavy of navel died by my side.
A tall crazy man ran and shrieked, ran and shrieked.
The day kept ending but night never came.
The day poured into my innards like an avalanche of sand.
Eight dead derelicts nipped at my dress.
And I gave my daughter birth.

"Hitarti kaftorei simlati," *Etz naga be'etz*, p. 7

.

[Die in me]

Die in me.
Who by fire and who by water and who by flood.[36]
I held out a rose to you.
I held my breath.
Die in me die in me die in me.
And darkness over the deep.

"Mut bi," *Etz naga be'etz*, p. 10

[The girl who drowned]

The girl who drowned deep in the well
and was lifted up soft and dripping
her face left deep in the well
to go with it.
The girl whose dresses would rustle
left her face deep in the well. The whiteness of her face
    deep in the well.
So thirsty was she,
my God.

"Hana'ara shetav'a betokh habe'er," *Etz naga be'etz*, p. 11

The Stripes of Joseph's Robe

The stripes of Joseph's robe [37]
were like rungs on the ladder of Jacob's dream.
The robe was hotter than sun moon and stars
sheaves spun off it when Joseph strode along.
In the pit he was as if in the arms of mother Rachel, she of the well,
overhead Ishmaelites journeyed, their bells tinkling
and on the camelhumps they carried him along
as in the heart of the sea
a camel flexes his neck like a long arm
and bracelets dance in Joseph's sight.
His mother hid the teraphim on the camel beneath her
pressing them to her like huge dolls
he touched them with his little finger
and they, thrusting a forefinger at him,
propelled him to Egypt.
The God of the Hebrews slept under him the whole way
like a huge rock gathered from many rocks.

"Hapasim bekhutonto shel yosef," *Etz naga be'etz*, p. 15

A Song for Jacob Who Removed
the Stone from Atop the Well[38]

He didn't know that I was Leah
And I—I was Leah.
Rachel, he said, Rachel, as the grass takes root in a ewe
so are the stems rooted in you.
The flocks of ewes bleated amidst our bedclothes,
the tent flaps stretched into the wind.
Rachel, he said, Rachel—
and my eyes, they were as weak
as the bottom of a dark swamp.

Into the yellow of my eyes the whites of his eyes melted.
The tent ropes tightened so
to hold onto the ground
when the wind blew from the palms of my hands.

He didn't know that I was Leah
and flocks of sons burst from my womb into his hands.

"Hazemer el ya'acov sheha'even me'al pi habe'er heisit," *Etz naga be'etz*, p. 14

Next to My God

Alone I sat next to my God
who misplaced me in the immense expanses
like a patch of sky,
and did not come to look for me.
I was laid out like one of the stones
while wind did not shift in me
and people did not rest ladders on me
to climb.
Alone I sat by my God
pressing my knees to my face
as when he created me and created the world
but not for chaos
as when I heard him creating me as the music of a flute
as a spare flame.

"Al yad elohai," *Etz naga be'etz*, p. 23

To Touch Him While He's Praying

To touch him while he's praying
maybe someone else's prayer
someone who for fear of his prayer
fled from here
and is still hiding somewhere.
To touch him while he's praying
and his body's moving like the tongue of a blue bell.
To touch him while he's praying
and his words—
without rhythm,
without echo,
pour over my face.

"Laga'at bo keshehu mitpalel," *Etz naga be'etz*, p. 24

[To hold your yearning]

To hold your yearning in my hand,
as if it were a child,
and to walk slowly with it,
into the fields.
At night
when I lean into the darkness so as not to trample it
the fields come to me all at once, all of them.
And I lack strength to fall on them.
At night
to give your yearning suck, as if it were a child
and to walk slowly with it into the fields.

"Et ergonkha lehaḥaziq beyadi," *Etz naga be'etz*, p. 25

And So I Followed Myself on the Paths

And so I followed myself on the paths
and the paths—they did not come with me.
Snow would cover me, or maybe it was fog
I heard steps treading in my tracks.
It was a soft little man who knew I wasn't there.
It was a soft little man who meant to erase my tracks.
Two dogs were with him and one owl.
And I'd leap after myself on the paths
and strong cold air caressed the breath of my mouth.
And I walked before myself along the paths
and the paths fled behind.
And I caressed the strong cold air
that caressed the breath of my mouth—and my teeth stiffened in me.

"Vekhakh halakhti aharei bashvilim," *Etz naga be'etz*, p. 27

[I was reborn]

I was reborn and ended in my womb
and my womb was slowly succumbing
in its silent passion to imprison me within.
I was born and ended in my womb,
no one ever came in me.
The barefoot birds would leave me in silence.
No one created me nor in me
the cells of my skin idly discharged themselves.

I did not give birth.
I was in heat biting at my womb
slowly crumbling between the palms of my hands.

"Shuv noladti," *Etz naga be'etz*, p. 29

Two Women Escaped

Two women escaped into night,
two women.
And night concealed them amid his stars.
And the women peeled off their heavy gowns
in whose folds they'd hidden many children.
And the women stiffly unbound their thin breasts
brimful of milk.
And night was their deliverer.
There was no skin on their hands
only sparse yellow hair.
A damp gloom covered the flesh of their thighs,
a moist quivering.
Night came nearer to them nearer and nearer
and passed them on among his stars.

"Shtei nashim nimletu," *Etz naga be'etz*, p. 57

Pleasure in Me

There's pleasure in me.
Wipe my lips.
In your childhood I was the fear in your windows.
In your old age I'll be a memory of every living thing.
Please don't banish me from your sight.
Look
the cypress in the courtyard proudly displays
a tender, elegant bite of my teeth.

"Edna bi," *Etz naga be'etz*, p. 68

A Circumcised Man and I

From *Haqolot likratam*
(The Sounds Towards Them, 1982)

A good-looking circumcised man grasps my shoulders,
he touches what's left of my wings.
—The two of us, remnants—to him I say—
I and my wings, you and your organ.
—The two of us, remnants—to him I say—
and all that exists in us is only beginnings and endings
we have no middle.
—O handsome man—to him I say—
we are middle, we have no beginning and no end.
The man grasps my hips.
We know that from them is our future
my ever broadening hips, my hips, an entire land.

"Ani ve'ish nimol," *Haqolot*, p. 9

King Solomon Who Stayed in the
Language of the Animals and Birds

King Solomon who stayed in the language of the animals and birds
and forgot the language of man
he'd sit on the Shulamite's[39] lap
and with a bleat he'd ask for the return of his tongue.
The Shulamite, hair coarse unkempt
would scratch his beard with her little finger
would plunge into his bleatings
"O parrot, O tiger, O cricket,"
she'd whisper to him
blending into the language of animals
fearing he might recall.
King Solomon lying on his back
bleating like a lamb
braying like a donkey
and the Shulamite sheds her garments.

"Shlomo hamelekh shenishar bisfat hahayot veha'ofot," *Haqolot*, p. 15

[I remained to guard the city]

I remained to guard the city
but the city arose and went off.
Whoever called the city by her name
will now call me instead,
a mother city am I,
to my south wilderness
to my north winter.

"Nisharti al ha'ir," *Haqolot*, p. 22

These Hills

I don't know whence these came to me
but I don't question them.
They're reclining in my bright armchairs
with lace napkins fastened to their peaks.
I'm so happy they came to see me
and I don't know if they're the Jerusalem hills or those of Naftali
I don't know if they've come from far away
effortlessly I cut a cake
and put crumb after crumb in their mouths
that my cake might come to the Jerusalem hills or those of Naftali
though I don't know whence they came to me.
O hills, O hills,
how you've ridden your horses all the way to me.

"Heharim halalu," *Haqolot*, p. 23

On a Jerusalem Hill Lies My Father

On a Jerusalem hill lies my father
among the crumblings of the dead.
Each has a name, inscribed in pale letters
and he flees from the name.
Father doesn't know when he was born
and when he breathed his last
and was it I who rose at night from his spurting
or was it he who had spurted.
The years of his death are more than those of his life
which was a slight fleeting solidity.
I cry over his grave
and my tears touch him like the autumn rain
an incomplete trickle
moving to the side of his full death.
For a moment I touched my father who was warm and merciful
and the hill touches him forever
my father takes pity on the stones on both sides
the crowdedness,
the fragile crumblings of the dead.
I was not his
only blood stirring in the veins.
And when they cast me upon the mount, in profile,
the hill, scorching, will gather me in,
its limestone earth will breathe me in
the years of my death will be more than the years of my life
and I won't know from whose spurting I arose
I'll not walk on the mount to view my father
because I had no father
I belonged only to the yellow mount
and at the blink of an eye I was sprayed by him
like lava, abandoning its source in a burst
in order to return to him.

"Al har birushalayim muna*ḥ* abba," *Haqolot*, p. 29

The Little Shepherdess

The little shepherdess
fields interwoven in her hair
and a ewe and a she-goat lick up
the crumbs of her dream.
The little shepherdess
whose slumber felled her in the field
and whose words rose up from within like a mist
and drifted to the ends of the pastures
scraps left in the tops of the stalk.
The elders of Zion came to investigate her[40]
to give ear to her sleep
as if to distant drumbeats
to peer into her with a fearsome eye
and she—like ancient scrolls in fire—
bursts.
The field is straw
and the sheep—cloud,
and she—like ancient scrolls in fire
bursts.

"Na'arat haro'im haqetana," *Haqolot*, p. 37

My God, the soul you have given me

My God, the soul you have given me[41]
flows within me like an hourglass
the earth in my high places touches the dust of my depths.
At times, at night, I remember
that in the ground the shadow is hidden for me
that from there it calls me by many names
that from there it prays to me
that I am its God the mighty and awesome
that I created it and I can kill it
that me it worships and to me turns in hope.
And when a man touches me and makes his seed flow
I am bound to someone else
who in silence digs deep tunnels
and for me digs even deeper.
For the pulsing seed in me is not of a man
dark and curly and tall
only from out of the dust have I taken it
and since then it keeps gushing in me
that I am its God and it is my God
the great, the mighty the awesome
I call unto it with many names
and by many names does it call me.

"Elohai neshama shenatata bi," *Haqolot*, p. 44

[All gathered here from afar]

All gathered here from afar
layer upon layer their faces
touch one, it falls
touch another, it comes
layer upon layer
as in Jerusalem earth
secreting many stones ample shadow
and congealed drops.
I want to touch a man—maybe he's a woman
weak armed in a flowing hairdo,
or a pale fingerless girl.
Fragile threads unravel after them
maybe they're a tail
or maybe one was torn from another
years ago, by some distance, or today,
here, with me.

"Kol ha'anashim kan," *Haqolot*, p. 47

The Last Will and Testament of the Sleeping Mother to Her Children

Children,
don't fall into sleep—
hold onto its edges.
I who taught you to sleep
I who wove you into lullabies for slumber
say:
My children, don't fall into sleep—
hold onto its edges.
I who taught you to sleep
want to teach you to wake
while I myself don't know how to wake.

"Tsava'at ha'em hayesheina liladeha," *Haqolot*, p. 50

Was I Born in the Light or in the Dark?

Was I born in light or in dark? Full of life, I turned her face
toward me.
At night I'm always pushed under a thin sheet
and hear muffled pounding under it
and someone opens a window and brings the news
that I was just born
or died
in a small stone house in Jerusalem.
You were born in light, Mother says
folding her hands on her stomach
and sighs.
You were born in light when the windows were open
and people in colorful clothes were bustling in the street
talking a lot
in many tongues, by many mouths.
Everything was open—says Mother,
eyes and shops and entrances of houses
I also was opened, says Mother,
into light.
I was born in light, I say,
so I close my eyes,
Mother, and stretch out my hands
to touch your face,
like a blind person coming close to you
in the dark.

"Ha'im noladti ba'or o ba<u>h</u>oshekh?" *Haqolot*, p. 58

Jerusalem, On the Verge of Drought

From Mishirei imot ha'even
(Poems of Stone-Mothers, 1988)

Jerusalem, on the verge of drought,
took the slender boy who'd walk in her
and her furrows will lead astray his feet, delicate as lace.
Jerusalem, a deep city, took the boy bereft of depths
to flood her banks
but he, my God, my God,
took me instead.

"Yerushalayim, al saf hayovesh," p. 79

Hear O Israel, Deep Within Our House

From *Maqom, namer* (Place, Tiger, 1994)

Hear O Israel deep within our house
The empty room lives all alone
What shall we do with it, the empty room
What shall we do with it, the empty room
Shall we go in and crowd between its walls
Or maybe offer it a sacrifice
Shall we shriek into its space or maybe shout with joy
Shall we open its doors or maybe lock them
Shall we call it cellar, shall we call it shrine
What shall we do with it, the empty room, what shall we do with it,
    the empty room
Shall we mess our hair in its honor, or comb it carefully
Shall we play hide-and-seek with it
until we grab hold and whisper: empty room, empty room
empty room.

"Shema yisra'el bema'amaqei beitenu," *Maqom*, p. 48

Caravans

In caravans the Hebrews return to their land.
Some of them limp. They were circumcised on the way.
Their names are changed. One will be called Tree. Another, House.
Another will be called Here.
Another, Now.
I, too, am a Hebrew girl among them.
Call me Whirlwind. Or Virginity. Or Sirocco.
Or Rivka and Miriam. Or Violin and Organ.

"Shayarot," *Maqom*, p. 56

To the South

Again the troops are streaming before me
on their way south
In the south, it's said, airy expanses of a hairsbreadth stretch out
a hairsbreadth, it's said, waits there
tense and bare
forsaken
They're all summoned to it
to rest with it and to move
the paths are filled with joy and metal and rasp and blast
The compass, too, revolves, its obstinacy reversed, and turns south
south
only there to rest and move
to rest and move at a hairsbreadth, in the south where nothing is
    beyond
like eyelashes on an eyelid close and open.

"Daroma," *Maqom*, p. 62

Happy Are They

Happy are they who mate with their parents
in the basement
clandestinely in a place of open eyes
and they're short-sighted their vision is blurred
only their necks are strong and sensitive antennae on their backs
and they mate with their parents at the rear
back and forth
again and again
like Ham with Noah, like his daughters with Lot
to impregnate themselves anew, or to block their being born at all
connecting their end to their beginning
an imprisoned fireball they are
until rest is found
until the strokes come to an end
until
and no more.

"Ashrei," *Maqom*, p. 72

[I was in that place]

From *Miqarov haya hamizrah,*
(Nearby Was the East, 1997)

I was in that place and the place gave me a hand.
On our trip I'd set out, but on our trip the place would stand back.
On our trip I envied how it stood back, and the place studied my steps.
There's nothing between us but size,
it turns out our size is the same.

"Bamaqom hayiti," *Miqarov,* p. 5

Jerusalem

After he called me by my secret name, "Jerusalem"
I was forced into exile. I went off weeping.
Children whose mother I'll never be again
were divided into egg and seed.
A throne on which I'll sit no longer
took root as a cedar.
A rod bare of snake and crocodile
hastily registered in the sand
my official, public names
that I might come back.

"Yerushalayim," *Miqarov*, p. 36

Don't Touch Me Just Now

Don't touch me just now.
Don't touch me just now.
At times like these my mouth can't chew
and a child can't be born of me.
The sense of touch is a burden just now.
Don't touch me. Don't touch me just now.
I don't even want the wind.
All my senses are a burden just now.
My flesh like an open pit.

"Al tiga bi akhshav," *Miqarov*, p. 62

Avner Treinin

BORN AT TEL AVIV in 1928, Avner Treinin lives today in Jerusalem where he is Professor of Physical Chemistry at the Hebrew University. His family background is worth noting. Treinin's paternal grandparents had lived in a territory known in our day as Belarus, in Vitebsk, the town where Marc Chagall grew up before leaving for Paris. At the age of nine, Treinin's father traveled with his grandmother on the Trans-Siberian Railroad to Harbin, China, to join Treinin's grandfather, who was seeking a livelihood in the Manchurian industrial center. Until his twenty-second year, Treinin Sr. lived in Harbin and then briefly studied medicine in Tomsk, Siberia.

When the Bolsheviks seized power, Treinin Sr., as the son of a family labeled bourgeois by the regime, was forced to leave the university. He returned to Harbin and, in 1921, emigrated to British-controlled Palestine where, he had been misinformed, it would be possible to study medicine in Jerusalem. That same year, Treinin's mother emigrated to Palestine. His parents met and married in Tel Aviv. Treinin Sr., unable to continue his medical studies in what had so long been a neglected Ottoman dependency, became a laborer roaming with his wife and four sons from place to place in search of a living—working in the orchards, paving roads, and for seventeen years, up to the War of Independence in 1948, employed in the Dead Sea potash fields.

Two years after Treinin's birth, the family moved to Jerusalem where the youngster received most of his early education. He was enrolled at the Takhkemoni School, studied at the celebrated high school Gymnasia Ha'ivrit, and joined the left-leaning Hashomer Hatza'ir (Young Guard) movement. During the 1948 war he served in a scientific unit and a year later married Rivka Shechter. Treinin went on to study Physical Chemistry at the Hebrew University; he also taught chemistry at the prestigious Rehavia Gymnasium and later at the University as well. Earning his bachelor's degree in 1954, he was awarded a Ph.D. in 1958 and spent 1958–59 in advanced research at Cambridge University. In 1971 he achieved the rank of Full Professor in Jerusalem. Treinin has held a Visiting Professorship at Brandeis University and, in 1973–74, was a Visiting Scientist at the United States Army Laboratory in Natick, Massachusetts. He has also produced much scientific writing and published textbooks in his field.

※ Short stories were the first literary works that Avner Treinin published. He was a student when he wrote his first story in 1947. During the War of Independence he met the poet T. Carmi who was assigned to the same military unit. It was his relationship with Carmi that led Treinin to turn to poetry. Treinin has been prolific as a poet, publishing nine collections between 1957 and 1996. Many of his poems have been translated into other languages.

Treinin's poetry reflects a mind conversant with numerous fields of knowledge. His poems range over the Hebrew Bible, contemporary Israeli literature, English literature, the Classics, Greek philosophy, Roman military annals, medieval and modern Jewish history, world geography, mathematics, and modern science. His academic education in science has contributed richly to his poetry, while other aspects of Treinin's Weltanschauung bespeak a large concern for the preservation of the planet, a healthy ecology, dying lakes in various regions of the world, and the stubborn Arab-Israeli conflict.

In a more personal vein, Treinin deploys a variety not only of themes, but also of styles and structures in his work. The Holocaust has a dominant role, though not always explicitly. The title poem of his 1991 collection, *The Memory of Water*, portrays a casual swim in a pool: the man touches the woman's thigh; fun and sensuality come together. A snake slips into the pool—the idyll is suddenly suffused with fear. The oppositional experience warns that distress or disaster may appear at any time. In the same poem, Treinin pictures cheap red kosher laundry soap with its menorah logo and a purification pallet, symbolic in Jewish tradition of blood, a Jewish home destroyed, death. Many of Treinin's poems demonstrate the oppositional structure.

Throughout the 1991 collection, water is the major theme. In "Pantha Re"—Heraclitus' notion of everything being in constant flux—Treinin alludes to the story of Noah's Ark; he expands the biblical myth by combining memory with water, even to the point of asserting that actually "water remembers"—alluding to a pseudo-scientific notion about water. Treinin also identifies water as a magical Wizard of Separation, a Wizard of Survival and Permanence. In the poem entitled "Lakes," the poet equates his own bitterness with Egypt's Bitter Lake in memory of a relative of his, a soldier fallen at the Suez Canal. Treinin renames it "Lake of Tears"—inevitably a reminder of the several cycles of Israel's wars.

Treinin's feeling for ecology enables him to paint many landscapes; he enjoys the beauty of the roses, pine, ivy, the "languid leaves" on the Giv'at Ram campus of the Hebrew University; the flaming bronze of Vermont foliage and the stones of Jerusalem. He makes the reader aware of his pleasure in walking amid Jerusalem's lovely, peaceful, ancient Sanhedrin graves—tombs of prominent talmudic sages—and hiking in the forest depths of the Judean hills.

Treinin, beginning his seventies, has assembled a virtual and actual archives of images in his poetry. Some are depressing, especially those of Holocaust scenes—looking through the window of a racing train, destination unknown; an ominously stopped clock; a speechless autist, nearly suffocated, an invalid, just barely connected to this world. The deaths of his parents and close friends are present in a number of his poems. Other images breathe life, escape and survival, a world pristine, unpolluted—secure in love, the joy of poetry, a rainbow, Paris, Jerusalem, a storm on Lake Lucerne—an abundance of expression: vivid emotion, linguistic control, humor, droll sarcasm. It is an extraordinary achievement, blending the aesthetic, the historical, and the scientific in one poetic "bundle of life."

[A few words on paper]
From *Hahzarot* (Reflections, 1988)

A few words on paper, actually on trees
and what's done to them, that is, the cutting,
the pulverizing, the pulp, a few words on the cellulose,
how it's separated, bleached, pressed,
made into paper, for these are words
on paper or on the hand writing
words on paper, how it turns gray,
ages, what's done to it,
silently, constantly, on disintegration,
destruction, decay, turning
into mulch, into trees, on what's done to them,
that is, back to paper, on the hand writing
paper, hand, here, now, noontime,
a bit cloudy, pleasant, looking at trees.

"Kama milim al haneyar," *Hahzarot*, p. 5

Facing a Journey

For my mother

("Everything was packed and ready as if going off on a journey,"
Hayim Be'er, *Feathers*)

Like an abscess with no way out, gnawing at us and rising
until the body's destruction that sweet sucking pain on the
border between soul and body,
which has no name except the soul's yearning
for something else that has no name,
as if found beyond the window, the highway,
the mountains, like a hidden destination of migrating birds,
hypnotized in their flow, how
they fly distances to Peru

in order to die. And like your mother so is my mother
packing her rags, preparing herself
for a long journey. And just as her body becomes emptied
this bag is filled with another pair of underwear
and one shoe. "Father and mother are waiting for me,"
she says, "and I have to go."

It turns out if so that the most private thing, like
the soul's yearning for something nameless,
is only a private instance within a general law,
bereft of compromise and any human relationship,
a law which packs all of us into the bundle of life,
but confounds us with delusions of the journey
as if from our soul comes the craving, departure
in a rowboat on the River Acheron

And not from the compulsions of some impassive force
which draws us to it like a bird in a magnetic
field or a field of another force,
and not only a tiny drop of hormone
is what sucks the soul so much

that it will quickly deflate
like air from a balloon, like the flushing of a toilet

At home or from the abscess that now bursts open.
But maybe they're right after all,
and awaiting us is not just a pit and a few bricks,
but there's also a place and there are those who wait—
if not beyond these mountains,
then beyond the mountains of darkness

"Liqrat masa," *Hahzarot,* pp. 14–15

From the Songs of an Autist

> I'm the gardener, I'm also the blossom,
> I'm not alone in the dungeon of my world.
> —O. Mandelshtam

1

What is a mother that you watch my mouth,
my eyes, my hand, I reach out and touch my mouth again,
wiping away a sticky crumb of foreign bread.
Don't you know, I'm still trying to escape
from a brutish breast covering my face, like a cushion
pressed down for strangulation. I'm still breathing and you'll not close
    off the air
circulating in my rooms. I'll again inhale through my nostrils like ducts
to the tank, from which I can't be cut off.
Like an invalid still connected to the world.

2

Within a covered skull, colored fragments
move about as in a box shifting and
reconnecting: an olive bud in the Valley of the Cross, a room
and a window, threads of light on the curtain, and you. And
another tiny shake scatters them and they become
glass splinters that were as if tossed here by mistake.
Who compels me to try again: Your fingers
come near me and try to touch, to grab hold.
This too has vanished. I'm touching myself.

3

She's so fast to pass. What pushes her
to the limit, where she's stopped and immediately
faces about and is already exhausting
all her strength and it's inertia alone that supplies the drive
to a complete turnabout to move back and forth.
But the routine, is it on this account she is restrained,
and again, like a pendulum that stops at last.

"Shirei autist," Haḥzarot, pp. 36–37

[Matter and anti matter]

Matter and anti matter. What remains
of the morning's algae, bubbles fainting
an egg just laid in the straw, straw-
berries sunflowers and corn, orange trees
and you, deep in the Sanhedrin graves.

Matter is like a wave that thrusts to its crest
it's already lost even the dim memory
of what its opposite was
until both opposites are mutually dissolved and all memory is lost.

Matter is energy that fades from
my organs and all the megatons that
are still stored in the end
won't be able to close
even an eyelid. Our Hiroshima
my love how gray and unimpressive.

To be or not to be is a question
that has no place at all. What's left
is a few equations of the new
physics and what remains of it.

"<u>H</u>omer ve'anti <u>h</u>omer," *Ha<u>h</u>zarot*, p. 104

Pantha Re[42]

From *Zikhron hamayim* (The Memory of Water, 1991)

And so, you won't step into the same river twice,
for the one who steps down won't be the one who's stepped down.
Even the dove did not return to Noah when the flood
subsided, for she returned but he was not the same innocent
Noah had been before he saw
with his own eyes the mountaintops and slopes without cities
without villages, a whole world without breath

Except God's awesome breath before
the waters were divided, then he became another man
naked and cunning—his sons sought in vain to cover him—
he crouched in his vomit from the wine he'd made
with his own hands he tarred a mini-ark, but alas
before that he lay in his vomit
if only to sweep from memory everything
that was swept away around him. If only his memory would be in
    the water

"Pantha Re," *Zikhron hamayim*, p. 7

The Memory of Water

It's doubtful I'll recall two or three years hence
how science was excited by a discovery, doubtful
today, that water remembers,
remembers your beauty that passed
through it that night in the pool,
how a tremor passed through you at the sight of the snake
slithering coiling at the bottom of the pool
its water recycled endless times since then

And your hands dripping on the washboard,
as the cheap laundry soap with its menorah logo
turned to a dark foam redder and redder
leaking now under the closed door
oozing over the pallet,[43] where undoubtedly
your body is laid not the body I still recall

Zikhron hamayim, p. 9

Where will the stream bear my little face?
(From "Songs of the Brook," Leah Goldberg)[44]

Leah, where has the stream borne your old face
With the memory of your little face borne off in the flow?
Abyss to abyss will call from the hills
and fall silent in the pipe. The faucet turns on its spindle,
and water rises in the glass, flowing from the walls

The house pours but doesn't dissolve. Pipe to pipe
the water grows darker. From the top of the waterfall storming falling
stopping in a space rusted sealed waiting
for salvation—turning on its axis and already
with the fullness of their freedom they're swept with all the rest
                                    right into the sewer's flow.

"Le'an yisa hazerem et panai haqetanim?" *Zikhron hamayim*, p. 10

[Water is the wizard]

Water is the wizard of separation, to separate so well
from the coasts, willows of lament, without wailing and lament
a tear separated from the eye, a bit salty,
not like pure water from the marble's surface parts
like water from water, molecule from molecule,

It's the wizard of survival, constantly
returning to the coasts, to the wadis, to the seas,
days and days from the clouds, in swollen furrows,
to a slab of polished marble under which you
lie, now, the marble beauty of your face

"Hamayim hem ashaf," *Zikhron hamayim*, p. 11

[The Yellow Sea and the China Sea]

The Yellow Sea and the China Sea carry you to Palestine.
Nineteen twenty one, your long jaundiced
face in the photo, the same surprised longing look
of beginning. Chinese, Hindus and Japanese
going up and down from the deck, the boat is Italian
Portuguese sardines, someone no longer alive
engraved his name for eternity in the wooden rail no
longer there, falling apart somewhere in a junkyard.
Stopping in Singapore at dawn, more Chinese Indians or Malaysians
going up and down, sacks of copra and rice,
with no waves panting in the hot mist a gulf like the tongue
of a filthy dog. Seaweed moving without belonging.
A rumor spreads through the deck that under
the grimy greasy calm the sea is swarming with sharks hungry
for blood. Then the two pop up, expressionless, ageless
they're eels with hardened muddy underwear, Chinese Hindus
or Malaysians, each face turns to look: a coin is tossed
into the water and they're already jumping off the deck and diving.
In the stupefying suffocating heat, screeches of seagulls
swooping down to the kitchen trash, fragments of organic matter,
one surfaces, in its mouth the metal shines
and a cunning smile. You're still a fervent believer:
"How can all this be, from the entire sea. And only one. His body dark
and slender, as though wrapped around her dreamlike body
rising from a conch. Pearl divers
at work. The conchs are empty. The divers are hungry."

"Hayam hatsahov vehasini," *Zikhron hamayim*, p. 15

Opposites Combine (Heraclitus)

The water that flowed in the orchard's hideout
is the water standing in the cells of my memory
as long as the blood flows in its vessels

In the cool water your thigh set afire
you were so cold still would understand
what had happened and would finally consent

and it still drives me mad
that these two opposites
        are joined together, so to speak.

> "Hanogdim zeh et zeh mit_h_abrim le'e_h_ad
> (Heraclitus)," *Zikhron hamayim*, p. 24

[In the strength of that trek]

In the strength of that trek into the grass momentarily
      hiding the sky above
its light goes on penetrating
      so purely filtered through its foliage
and the rush of the murky water
in the forest depths
      no beginning no time,
already starting to end

"Bekho'a<u>h</u> hahalikha" *Zikhron hamayim*, p. 25

Lakes

In memory of Yehuda Rosenfeld, who fell at the Suez Canal

The Great Salt Lake in Utah,
the Salt or Dead Sea in Israel,
icy Great Slave Lake and Bear Lake,
the lakes of borax and soda and bromides,
and hydrogen sulfide from the decomposing of what was burnt
and swept away, Lake Baikal, the Bardawil and the Bitter Lake
at Suez. And when the corner of the eye can hold no more
the Lake of Tears will drain into the ducts of the nose

"Yamot," *Zikhron hamayim*, p. 29

[Middle age well behind me]

Middle age well behind me this morning I gasp for breath
on the rise of pine at the edge of the Univer-
sity, as I step into a brake of twisting ivy
along with wild roses and languid attempts of leaves teased
into a flaming bronze which puts on a Vermont face
above the Jerusalem stones.
And the scenes flash by
as if through the window of a racing train
at the center of my brain on the screen,
the silent film stuck inside me
in the torrential sweep of a timepiece without hands
or with hands still stopped at 8:40
in Miss Havisham's clocks[46]—
and she, like a skeleton arrayed in bridal wreaths,
eternally seated in an armchair amid great expectations.

"Harḥeq begil ha'amida," *Zikhron hamayim*, p. 33

[The first of May]

The first of May '87, the anniversary of my father's death
from a disease or from natural causes (what's not natural
in a disease, starvation, gas, napalm,
artillery, and the other sophisticated deaths
devised by human nature?) and it was also
May Day, including "The Inter-
national," in short, a day of memory:
Climbing the mountain with a bouquet of flowers, the scenery
spectacular after a rainy year.
The Beit Zayit pond seen from above, a man-made
reservoir. The graves, too.

His death was relayed to me in New York and I tried so hard
to mourn. For before his final death he had died many early deaths.
This, too, is natural for one who lives long,
especially one who at nine had already undergone
so much change in a trans-Siberian railroad car,
on his journey from Vitebsk to Harbin.

After the funeral, with him already covered over
(two weeks earlier he'd sought in vain to cover himself
with every blanket in sight against the cold of
approaching death) I came to my mother, sitting
by herself and, with a wink, she told me
that Lonya (that's what she called him)
had gone out early that morning and still hadn't returned
and the devil alone knew where he was wandering.

"Ehad bemai '87," *Zikhron hamayim*, pp. 34–35

From "The Mud People"—
1.These Are the Chronicles]
From *Ma'alot Ahaz* (The Sundial of Ahaz, 1996)

"These are the Mud People," the bull neck and shaved head
spatters its contempt from the screen
on Jews, Blacks, and all the rest.
(He's not one of them not them*them*
because he's an earth-man from Savannah, Georgia.)
"These are the chronicles of humankind. A man and a woman in God's
    image
were created equally together in Chapter One. And in the Second
there's already a correction; the man emerges from the earth
and after him, a woman, hard as a rib.
Later, in the mire, maybe when the Flood receded,
then the Mud People were molded from water and dust,"

Which in winter fields, beneath the houses, the streets,
from mud to mud they wallow in torn shoes. And the heavens that
    burst
upon a cloud in black and as if by signal turned into
treetops starlings in the evening trees at the hospital,
howling drowning out the screams of those circling
in striped coats, back and forth between bed and bars
in the insane asylum at the entrance to my town,

Which with rocks in moss, moldy niches at the poorhouse,
like a mole in its burrow the old man's eyes surprised
at the gleams of dusty daylight, and puddles that bring back
the visions to me

"Anshei habotz," Ma'alot Ahaz, p. 9

Autumn Crocus

From mud to thorn my city wanders, turbaned with a wall,
enveloped like the cowl of monks stealing out of the Armenian Quarter
to wander in the alleys, to sin and atone

Breaches of lust whose first arousal is
the late summer squills, thin candles, whose erection
is from a tangled crown of thorns, and now

With no prelude, in white, virginal pink, from
abstinent earth to autumn's ejaculation of rain.

"Sitvanit," *Ma'alot Ahaz*, p. 10

From "Engraved"—3. Tea

The sun melted the day and itself melted
and both were hammered out
cast together into the green salt pool.
Now in the dark the carnalite crystals precipitate.

The workers' kitchen. Galevsky at the radio dial searching
for Russia. Noisily angering all his enemies,
the enemies of the Revolution. One after another
he sends them off, with Russian curses, to kiss his ass.

A snort of words, incomprehensible, and what are the signs,
and how did they get here, to this lowest spot,
and suddenly, words of longing, already smothered.
Lying beyond the window the sea is dead.

My father's fingers grasp a glass of tea.

"Tei," *Ma'alot Aḥaz*, p. 19

Beauty

This morning I saw your face for the first time.
I don't know who you are and doubt I'll ever know
but I knew you weren't always so
beautiful. Also the strong vulgar lipstick fit your alabaster
skin so well. O you were so beautiful
as I passed by your face multiplied by dozens of screens
in the electronic shops, 14th Street,
among bazaar bargains, perfumes, beauty aids

Saragossa Coffee Shop, crooked dice players,
cards, the nauseating smoke of deep fried
and grilled meats, sugared almonds, a Salvation Army
Temple, a filthy swarming sidewalk,
ziti for $2.75, an agèd nun so slowly
to the convent of St. Zita, the New York Armory
the National Guard 42nd Infantry Division,
clothing, clothing, children, all for a dollar
Your head, its white silk pillowcase, a bouquet of daffodils
the black luster of the coffin, its engravings, its red padded
cover, falling over your face

"Yofi," Ma'alot Ahaz, p. 26

[In a book on boredom]

In a book on boredom—it's called "Boredom" (I've
not been able to read it through to the end)—
I found an explicit statement
that the concept boredom came into use
only in the eighteenth century
and I'd naively thought it absolutely familiar
even to a dog when its gaping jaws turn into a yawn
detached and hanging in the air like a rising cloud of flies
falling back to land on the face
of a boy idly tearing the wings off one:
how long can it survive
without the ability to fly—

buds of scientific curiosity (whole fruits we had the luck to taste)
such as Vespasian conqueror of Judea had
demonstrated earlier when he stood by the Asphalt Sea,
the Ancient Sea, and to pass the time
ordered his captives, chained to one another,
tossed into the heavy waters: to measure precisely
the time it took them to surface.

"Besefer al hashi'amum," *Ma'alot Ahaz*, p. 35

[In the display windows of the Village]

In the display windows of the Village like the prostitutes in Amsterdam
you see them mostly in muted neon light revealing a destiny, reading
    palms and cards, in the stars or in coffee, a crystal ball by their side.
A skeptical smile conquers the fear facing them,
but don't worry: not in these mouths what he'd seen at night in his
    chamber
in the city of Salon in Provence in the sixth century of this
second millennium; Michel de Nosterdam on the eve of the third
    millennium:

> "In one thousand nine hundred ninety nine and seven months the
> Great Fearsome King will descend from the heavens and
> resurrect Genghis Khan;
>   and later as before war will reign in joy."

In your palm I see many good years, but beware.
From the line of Apollo it's becoming clear: you tend to gamble a bit.
Lines digress from the line of the heart: you tend to womanize a bit.

I look to the stars: your constellations[47] and your mate's, they, Pisces
    and Aquarius,
are like fish in an aquarium, but you have luck—mazal[48]—
the problem will be solved.
And there's more in your palm: a malady, imminent, difficult, but you'll
    overcome it.
You'll also have money problems, but it will all turn out well—

Clear words acceptable to both mind and heart.
Maybe they're like the words a woman prophesied to your nephew
    Yehuda Leib, here in the photo, on the right, a fortune teller
in Warsaw in the 1930s.

"Behalonot hara'ava baVillage," *Ma'alot Ahaz*, p. 37

[On Waverly Street]

On Waverly Street there's a bookstore called "Three Lives."
One life for Adam, between the Tree of Knowledge and the Tree of
    Life,
and for Jacob two lives, Jacob and Israel.
How many lives does a human being have and what does he do with
    them?
And what's your view of life, of life's sanctity, let's say?
Death to abortionists, death to murderers of the unborn!
What is there amid the swarms of people, by the foul
roadside—a pile of garbage? a human being?

In Hebrew, the word "God"[49] is plural, not one, Jesus is his son.
How Elohim saved Jimmy Swaggart, their evangelist son,
from the error of his ways.
Jimmy Swaggart televangelist, what a lust for life,
how he arose from among the errant
and ran again across the screen

To be sure not on such a respectable channel (sandwiched
between a pair of porno films) but two years ago I saw him
running out-of-doors before a congregation of hardpressed,
tearful Porto Ricans, he was going around in circles and sobbing
how Jesus has saved his life and now he's a different person.
And how wondrously the Porto Rican translator,
who ran after him, rendered each and every sob.

"Birehov Waverly," Ma'alot Ahaz, p. 41

[Death is the peak of democracy]

Death is the peak of democracy. Socks, a book, a hand
waking this morning upon your breast, God, what
a sensational bow, and already scirroco,
a slice of bread is the peak of ants

At the edge of summer shpritz of the squirting cucumber, caper
thorns, and what else, also move toward decay.
Plastics live longer, a juice bottle, rust

Piles and piles of shit, a scrap of newspaper
for thinking people. Carbon hydrogen, and what else,
oxygen, sulfur and ammonia—all alike
without prejudice, total equality

of atoms. Time's victory is the victory of
matter over your face, water clouds over the rainbow.
A rainbow will inherit a rainbow, not you your life.

"Hamavet hu pisgat hademocratia," *Ma'alot Ahaz*, p. 48

[The stars Abraham counted]

The stars Abraham counted were in his eyes
which saw other heavenly stars of Abrahams
before him. Many years the light of these
distant stars wandered,
before reaching Abraham with the light of stars

which had perished long before his birth.
Nor did he see the newborn stars
for no sign of them has arrived even now.
Like the signs from the Creator on high which he sent

us so that we'll know at last whence we came and whither we go
and this before he vanished, signs which might
arrive sometime after we'll have vanished.

"Hakokhavim sheAvraham safar," *Ma'alot Aḥaz*, p. 58

[Today too Gavriel is depressed]

Today too Gavriel[50] is depressed.
The ongoing whiteness of the page
the whiteness of a face revealed to him
yesterday from the ambulance stretcher.

Like a diapered baby an old woman's
stare hasn't left you.
Were you a final image
imprinted unintelligibly
    on the retina of a stranger's eye

Or was it a look of wonderment
to find you here facing her
instead of in Samarra[51] for your appointment—
until the doors were flung open for her
and she was carried off

A frightful sob of sirens
in the endless traffic flow
of The Bronx, it's the River Acheron.

"Gam hayom Gavriel m'dukka," *Ma'alot Ahaz*, p. 71

Notes

1   R. B. Kitaj, *First Diasporist Manifesto* (New York, 1989), p.13.

2   William Carlos Williams, *Collected Poems, 1921–1931,* with a preface by Wallace Stevens (New York, 1934), p. 2.

3   William Styron, "Foreword," *The Human Experience: Contemporary American and Soviet Fiction and Poetry* (Santa Barbara, 1989), p. xvii.

4   Haim Gouri, "Kmo Beirut," *Ha-ba aharay* (Tel Aviv, 1994): see also Gouri, *Words in My Lovesick Blood* (Detroit, 1996), trans. S. F. Chyet, pp. 220–21.

5   V. S. Naipaul, "Reading & Writing," in *The New York Review of Books,* February 18, 1999, p. 14.

6   "Hovot halevavot," a medieval Spanish ethical tract by Bahya ibn Pakuda.

7   Joshua 11:4.

8   See Bertolt Brecht, *The Threepenny Opera,* Act One, Scene Two (Jenny's Song).

9   Cf. Esther 1:10.

10   The "north" here alludes to the rich northern suburbs of Tel Aviv.

11   Cf. Ezekiel 37.

12   Cf. Lamentations 5:16, "The crown has fallen from our head," used now as the formal announcement of a death.

13   Amos 2:13, 15; 5:19; Jonah 4:5–7.

14   "Dessert," concluding the Passover ritual meal (Seder). See Mishna, Pesahim 10:8.

15   Cf. Judges 16:9.

16   Just before the outbreak of war with Egypt and Syria.

17   A popular song of the 1950s. In the song, *Tzena* refers to girls going out to see their soldier boyfriends.

18   A Ramat Hasharon family killed in a highway accident while touring the United States (*Ma'ariv,* 21/7/92).

19   Song of Songs 2:5.

20   The evil archdeacon in Victor Hugo's novel *The Hunchback of Notre Dame.*

21 Cf. Genesis 18:1–2.

22 The original term *ba'oholot* is derived from the mishnaic tractate *Oholot*, which deals with the Jewish laws of purity in the home. The text states a "tent" (*ohel*) instead of the "home," but the connotation is maintaining a kosher home and knowing its laws.

23 A town in Eastern Algeria.

24 A medieval rhymed prose story replete with adventures and magical events.

25 A stringed instrument played by the Bedouin, usually in the evening around a campfire.

26 The ancient Akkadian goddess of the sea.

27 Ernst Cassirer, *An Essay on Man: An Introduction to a Philosophy of Human Culture* (Garden City, 1953), pp. 183, 185–86.

28 A Zen paradox or question.

29 Cf. Genesis 46:28; 47:27.

30 A Jerusalem cemetery.

31 Cf. Babylonian Talmud, Ta'anit 29a; the legend of the keys to the Second Temple, destroyed by Titus, thrown into the air—heavenward—by the priests.

32 An ancient piece of jewelry.

33 A medieval liturgical poem.

34 1985.

35 Cf. 2 Samuel 20:1;1 Kings 12:16.

36 Cf. "Unetaneh toqef" prayer in the Day of Atonement liturgy.

37 Cf. Genesis 37.

38 Cf. Genesis 29.

39 Cf. Song of Songs 7.

40 Cf. Apocrypha: Susannah and the Elders.

41 Cf. daily morning prayer.

42 "Everything in flux" (Heraclitus, 540–480 B.C.E.).

43 Used in Jewish tradition for purification of a body before burial.

44 (1911–70) beloved poet and Professor of Comparative Literature at the Hebrew University of Jerusalem.

45 Cf. I Kings 19:8.

46 In Charles Dickens's 1861 novel *Great Expectations*.

47 In Hebrew: *mazalot*.

48 In Hebrew, *mazal*, a planet, also denotes luck.

49 *Elohim*.

50 Estonian-born Gavriel Preil (1911–93), who wrote splendid poems in Yiddish and Hebrew, lived most of his life in New York.

51 John O'Hara's 1934 novel, *Appointment in Samarra*.

Both Warren Bargad and Stanley Chyet are natives of Boston, Massachusetts, and Boston Latin School alumni. Warren Bargad earned his undergraduate degree from Harvard University and his Ph.D. degree in Hebrew Literature from Brandeis University. Stanley Chyet graduated in 1952 as a member of Brandeis University's first class; he holds rabbinical ordination and a Ph.D. degree in American Jewish History from Hebrew Union College—Jewish Institute of Religion.

In addition to their other publications, the two collaborated on *Israeli Poetry: A Contemporary Anthology* (1985), published initially in hardcover and then in paperback by Indiana University Press.

Dr. Bargad recently retired as Director of the Center for Jewish Studies at the University of Florida in Gainesville and as a senior member of the University faculty. Dr. Chyet recently retired as Professor of History and Literature at the Hebrew Union College in Los Angeles; he will continue as assistant to the President of the Skirball Cultural Center and as Secretary to the Cultural Center Board of Trustees.